Re-inventing the Landscape:
contemporary painters and Dorset

Vivienne Light

Canterton Books

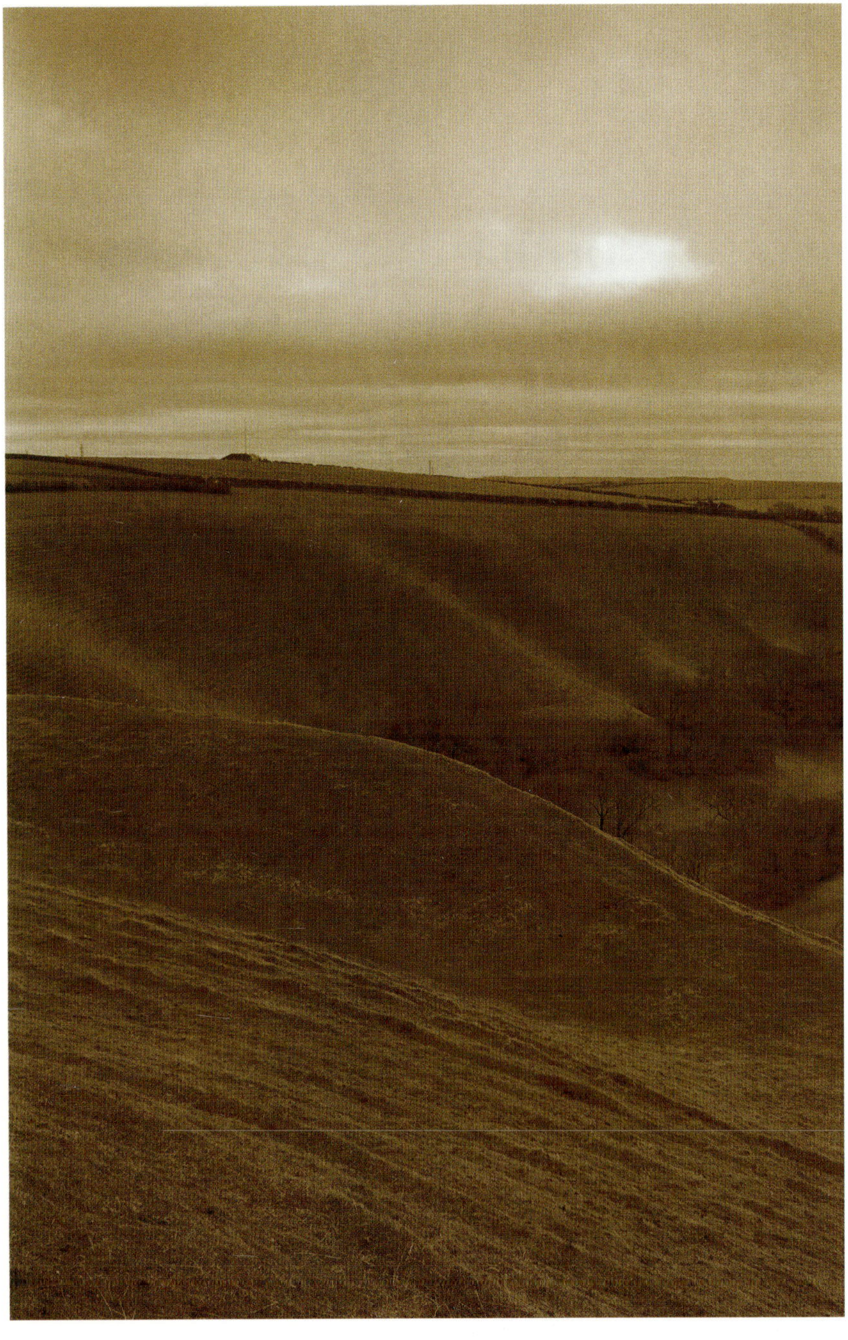

Eggardon Hillfort

Re-inventing the Landscape:
contemporary painters and Dorset

ISBN 0-9541627-0-6

Published by Canterton Books
Forest Ford
Brook
Hampshire
SO43 7HF
UK

www.cantertonbooks.cjb.net

Printed by Brown & Son
Crow Arch Lane
Ringwood
Hampshire
BH24 1PD
UK

Book Design Sarah Jane Jackson

First Published December 2001

CONTENTS

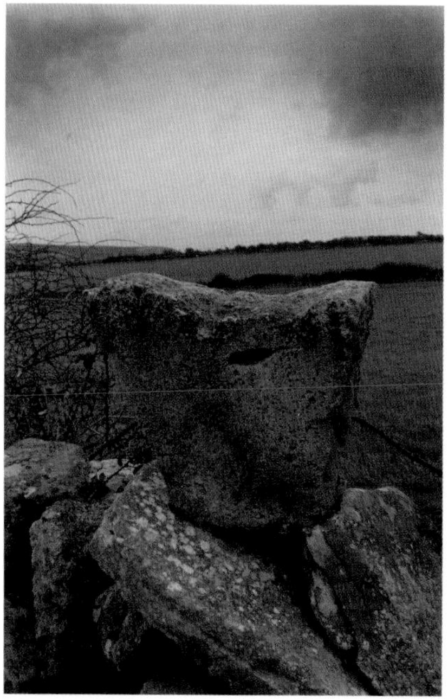

Purbeck

For Paul

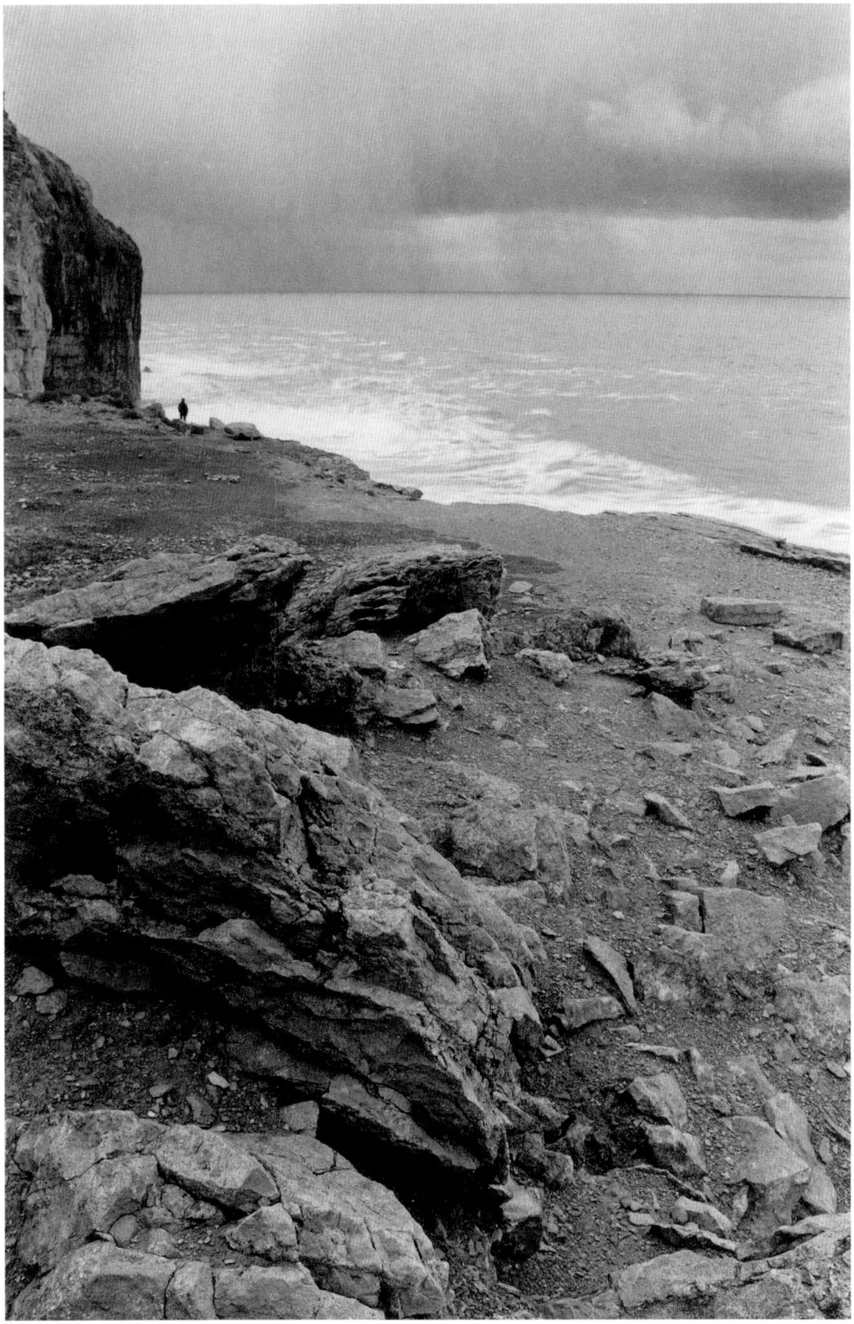

Solitary Figure

PREFACE
Simon Olding

Throughout the 1990s, when I held the post of Director of the Russell-Cotes Art Gallery and Museum in Bournemouth, I proposed that we should reintroduce a vigorous programme of displaying contemporary art. This had been a feature of activity at the Russell-Cotes in the 1920s, 30s and later. Important and very popular shows featuring the works of Paul Nash, Liz Frink, and many other artists with Dorset associations were programmed. Reinvigorating this approach for a later decade brought me into close partnerships with many of the artists whose work is described with such clarity and elegance in Vivienne Light's eagerly awaited book.

Within this community of Dorset artists there are some clear affinities, and a common language of expression. The subtle chalk light of Dorset illuminates Peter Joyce's lyrical and restrained abstract summaries of cliff and seascape, as it does (in a more expressionistic manner) a highly wrought canvas from Brian Graham. Partly because of the important new role of the Russell-Cotes in presenting the work of Dorset artists, partly because of the collective demonstration of their significance through the emerging Dorset Art Weeks, and partly because of a new confidence in teaching fine art, led with quiet but influential determination by Jim Hunter at the Arts Institute at Bournemouth, Dorset artists have worked with a new found confidence. The infrastructure of the visual arts has developed too, with impressive lottery-funded projects at the Russell-Cotes and the new Study Gallery in Poole.

Over this decade, we have seen the emergence of a community of individuals, whose work is grounded in the description of landscape, and that very particular landscape of Dorset, with its still remote and primeval edge to the sea, and the archaeologically rich pattern of chalk slopes. Some of the artists whose work is described here have settled in Dorset, but brought an international perspective to their description of landscape (Hubbard and Brewster, for example). George Dannatt has maintained his long-held association with the St Ives School, and there are other strong affiliations with Cornish painting, for example in works by Vanessa Gardiner and Pádraig Macmiadhacháin.

Indeed there are potent physical similarities in standing both at the headlands of St Just and the Isle of Purbeck: the sense of being remotely at the edge of sea and land from a high vantage point is strong in both locations. These are evocative and romantic places. Alastair Michie looks in forceful detail to describe the cliffs of Purbeck in allusive calligraphic marks. Robin Rae takes a more figurative approach to coast scenes, and Robert Woolner is occupied both with ancient made landscape forms and the effects of light and space around the landscape. Alex Lowery has focussed his work almost exclusively on the settlement of West Bay, a place 'imposed on the land'.

For the painters of the Dorset landscape, remoteness and 'antiquity' have been captured in an essential form-the description of place in an abstract visual language. Perhaps we cannot describe this body of work as that of a contemporary Dorset school. But we can see, I believe, evidence of a high degree of shared understanding and respect of place, within a community of individuals living and working in close proximity, who have an intelligent critical understanding of each other's artistic practice.

Kingston Russell Stone Circle

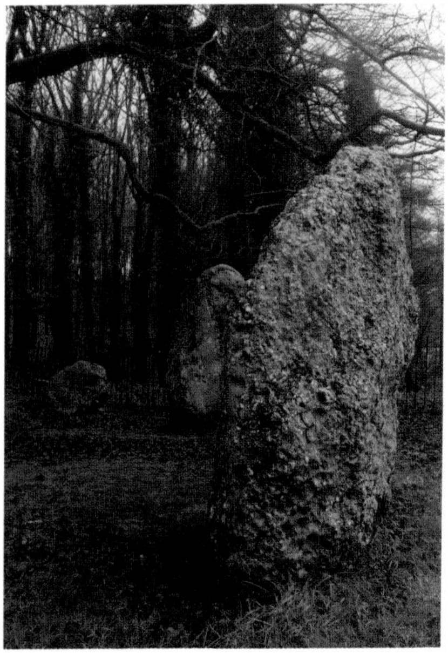

INTRODUCTION
Vivienne Light

Since the early 1990s, I have become increasingly aware of the work of several painters for whom the Dorset landscape is a key subject. This is not to say that these painters work exclusively with the Dorset landscape, but rather, that over a period of time, it is a subject to which they often return. Most of their painting tends towards the abstract; their interest lies not so much in topographic realism as in conveying a sense of place. Their central concern may be described as how to hold onto 'place' once the figurative scaffolding is removed.

There are undoubtedly other painters who could have been included in this volume but any such venture is constrained by space and time. Hopefully, there will be opportunities to make this good through further volumes and also widen the remit to include contemporary sculptors such as Mary Spencer Watson and Don Potter. There is room also for a retrospective look at the work of Reynolds Stone, Paul and John Nash, Elizabeth Frink and others who had (and in an important sense still have) close connections with Dorset.

Dorset has an illustrious record regarding artists who have worked with its landscape: from the late seventeenth and early eighteenth century through to the present day. Twentieth century names include not only the above, but others such as Stanley and Gilbert Spencer, Henry Lamb, Augustus John, Roger Fry, John Piper, Frances Hodgkins and John Craxton.

Dorset has always been a rural county. For much of its history it has been a place of isolated communities and small towns; nothing sophisticated, few exceptional events. An unpretentious place, it has guarded both itself and its landscape. In the last few decades, with the many European directives and incentive schemes, it has perhaps been subjected to more change than it has experienced before. However, the heart of the land remains constant and essentially the same. Fundamentally, the primeval landscape of Dorset continues to exist. This is very much evidenced in the dramatic photographs taken by Martin Hampton.

These photographs catch at the timelessness and sculptural qualities found within the Dorset landscape. It is said that Dorset's geology is richer and more diverse than that of any other county in Britain. Limestone, chalk, greensand, shale, clay and marble all contribute to a structural fabric which has the power to attract the landscape painter like a moth to a lamp. Erosion has sculpted much of this land and coast, leaving contours of smooth round hills, hard prominent plateaux, folded valleys and a coastline alternately even and irregular. Inland, physical features are softened by copses and woods, heathland and scrub, sandy plains, arable and dairy land and, no matter where you are, the sky seems always high and open, the light clear.

Dorset is an ancient place. Early Mesolithic camps were sited along the coast where the climate was relatively mild. These sites, and many others like it, confetti the landscape of Dorset. Aerial photographs reveal a multitude of long barrows, disk barrows, circles, and hill forts. Some ancient sites, such as the Iron Age fort of Maiden Castle, are well known to the general public, while others, such as The Grey Mare and Her Colts, tend to be known only to local people, archaeologists or other particular enthusiasts. To many painters such sites are atmospheric places, having a presence, and, at certain times, a strangeness, which they find difficult to define.

In the Middle Ages the population of Dorset was probably greater than it is today. Evidence of medieval agriculture is still to be found in strip-lynchets; the narrow terraces which rib the sides of many Dorset hills. The cutting of stone on Portland and Purbeck has been a long time activity, and still continues today, if, to a much lesser extent. Over years it has helped shape, with quarries, ledges and cliffs, the distinctive profiles of the 'Isles' of Portland and Purbeck.

Perhaps it is the coastline, more than any other part of Dorset which draws the painter, and Dorset has indeed a very special coastline. The proposal for it to become a 'World Heritage Site' justly reflects its uniqueness. On the Isle of Purbeck one can be surrounded on three sides by the sea, and the quality of light is truly exceptional. Here are the architectural and geometric ledges and cliffs of Winspit, Kimmeridge and Dancing Ledge. These can be awesome places. To the West lies Lulworth Cove, a contrasting quiet, smooth-rimmed bay, while nearby is Stair Hole, a long sinewy cliff made of crumpled stone. A little further along lies Durdle Door with its limestone arch straddling the sea. The coast then leads away to Ringstead Bay and the sands of Weymouth before turning outwards to the Isle of Portland. Portland has an atmosphere which can be described as both desolate and magnificent; it is stone through and through. The village of Chiswell, at the base of Portland hill, marks the abrupt start of the Chesil Bank, a bank of shingle which stretches eighteen miles down the coast to West Bay, passing en route the exotic tropical gardens of Abbotsbury. At West Bay, once known as Bridport Harbour, the Chesil ends but the Dorset coast continues to the sandstone cliffs of Golden Cap. Finally, at Lyme Regis, the happy hunting-ground of palaeontologists, Dorset reaches the red borders of Devon. Such a coast is indeed a natural heritage site and a magnet for painters.

I lived close to the Chesil Bank for the early part of my life. At that time my father farmed at Kingston Russell, near Winterbourne Abbas. We lived in a Portland stone farmhouse surrounded by the flint-specked chalkland of West Dorset. From a very early age I recognised that I lived in a special place. I believe that the painters, who make up this book, equally recognise that they live in a singular place. As I visited their studios, some of which were in relatively 'hidden' places, so their separation from each other and each other's work, became evident. However, as John Donne once wrote: 'No man is an island, entire of itself' (*Devotions*). Perhaps the one uniting factor between them, besides a love of place, is a desire, in their painting, to 'make known' something beyond the more obvious, what Nash referred to in his own work as, the *genius loci*, the spirit of place. He also, however, talked about 'the point of departure', which was when a painting took on a life of its own. Thus, any painting can be said to be the result of a symbiotic relationship between the 'spiritual' and 'actual', with successful completion depending on a process of both invention and re-invention.

Through their paintings, all of these artists offer us new ways of seeing place and landscape. Through their words, reflected in these essays, we also glimpse the worlds within which they live and work.

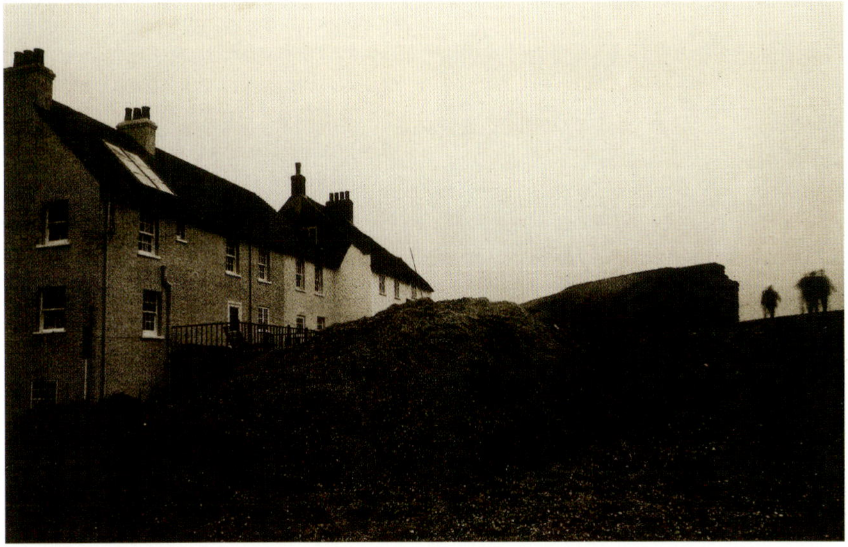

West Bay

MARTIN HAMPTON

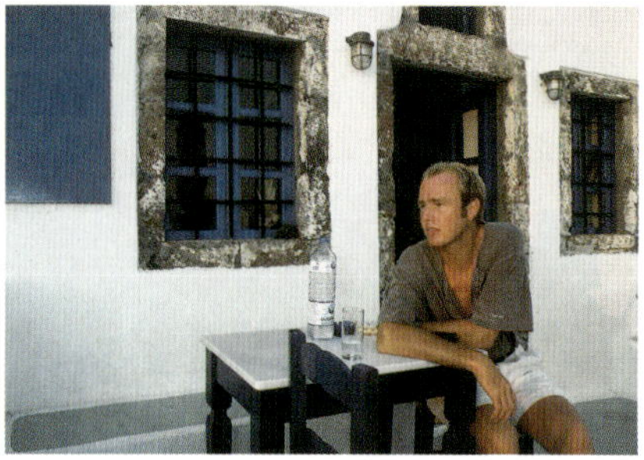

Martin Hampton (b.1962) lectures in photography at the Leica Academy in Athens, where he lives with Evangeli and their son, Jocelyn. He has a BA in Cultural Studies from the University of East London and a BA in Photography from the University of Westminster. He has been involved in further education and training for some years. Whilst acknowledging the vast potential of digital technology and multimedia, particularly in helping to articulate the concerns of under-represented groups, he still loves the beauty and mystery that comes with the historical processes of print-making.

Martin Hampton is involved in a wide variety of photographic projects and exhibitions. For *Change*, he developed a series of monochrome photographs of synthetic objects transformed by the sea. This visual metaphor was supported by text which explored 'the process of change at the heart of society'. For *Car Whispers,* he developed silver-gelatin, gold-toned photographs of car wrecks; wrecks abandoned by the side of the road in the Peloponnese. These photographs were again supported by text, in this case stories about car ownership and popular culture.

At the present time, he is working on *Marathona: a battlefield in transition*. For this project he is making landscape and documentary photographs which record Marathona's archeological heritage and unique topography of plain, mountains and sea-coast. In supporting text, he articulates the concerns of local people about their future as the area is transformed for the Olympics.

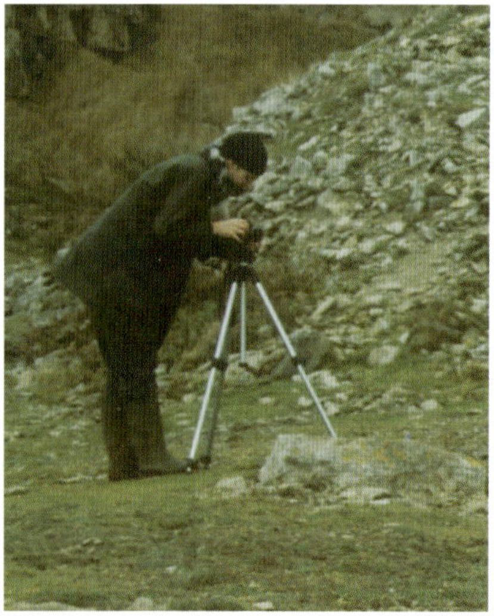

As regards the photography for *Re-inventing the Landscape,* it was on two, overcast, drizzly days in December, between Christmas and New Year, that Martin set out with the author, and his photographic equipment, to take the photographs which appear in this book. Perhaps little more needs to be said about those special days ... I think the resulting images speak for themselves.

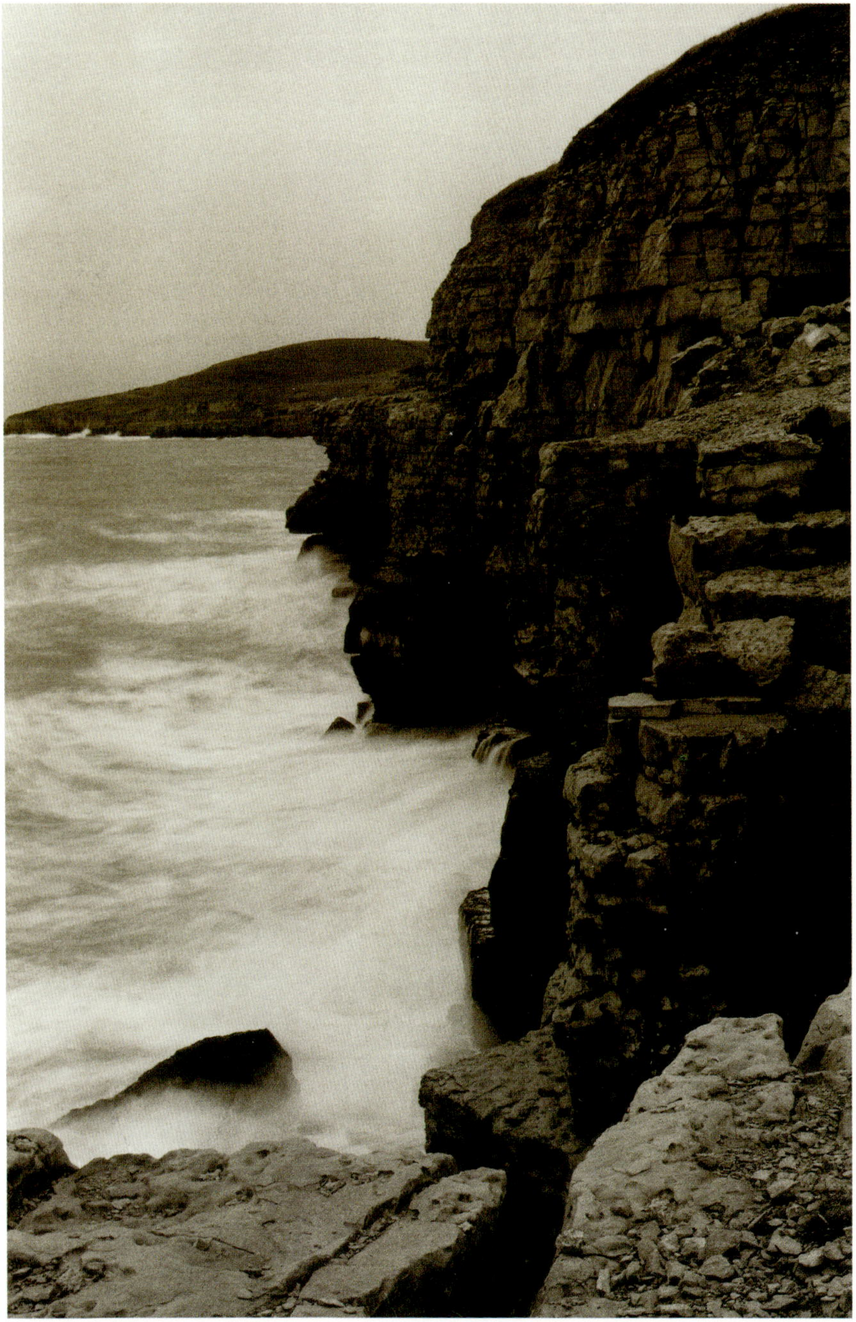

Winspit

MARTYN BREWSTER

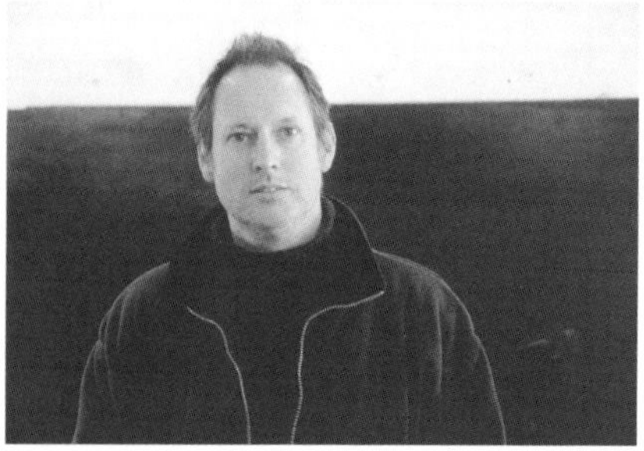

For Martyn Brewster it is a ten-minute walk from his house to the sea; a place of high cliffs, beach and open sky. On overcast days, mists and sea-fog hang limp in the air, dissolving land forms and creating eerie spaces. On clear days, strong white light sharpens coastal faults and accents the movement of water and waves. Brewster's concern as a painter has long been with the dynamic restlessness of nature, the changing quality and strength of light induced by time of day, the seasons and the elements. Although Brewster's painting is to do with abstraction, tonality, colour and the material substance of paint itself, his inspiration comes from nature's forms, space, and light.

From the East Cliff, most of Bournemouth bay can be seen, and from here Brewster has the choice of walking in either one of two directions. Eastward lies the golden promontory of Hengistbury Head, with the Isle of Wight lying a short distance away across the water, while westward, are Poole Harbour, Brownsea Island and the sands of Studland and Swanage. Along the cliff path there are woodland interjections known locally as chines. These are precipitous narrow spinneys which are covered with Scots fir, laurel and spruce. Paul Verlaine (1877), a French poet, described these chines as 'starting high up against the sky' before twisting and zigzagging down to the shore.[1]

Bournemouth was Thomas Hardy's Sandbourne, 'a place where the pines murmured in precisely the same tones as the sea', a sea that was 'near at hand, but never intrusive'[2]. The town has grown from an original scattering of sea-side villas and terraces to a place which today embraces the architecture of modern corporate buildings and cut-through roads. Yet in spite of increased urbanisation the bay itself maintains a separate life and appeal of its own. On warm days the sands become the province of visitors, swimmers and ice-cream vendors. On dark nights however, there comes an unquiet stillness with

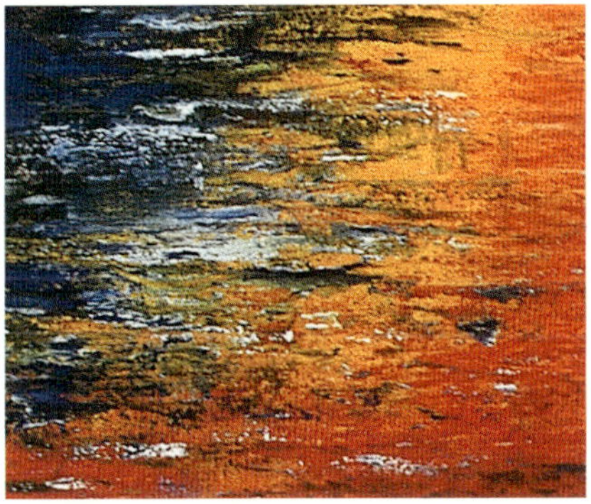

Detail *Night and Day Quartet* (2000)

the sounds of music, people and cars being somehow distanced. As the lights on the streets and in buildings are switched on, coloured reflections ripple across the water, adding an almost magical dimension to the scene.

As a Fine Art student at Brighton (1971-74) Brewster lived on the flat Sussex coast. He loved living there for the light, but did not find the coastland inspiring. In contrast, when he moved to Bournemouth in 1988, he found the Dorset coast striking and powerful in imagery. "There is so much going on, so many angles, shapes and colours, forms and light changes. It is wonderfully dramatic even when the weather is relatively calm."

Hengistbury Head is a favourite place of his. It is a heath and scrub peninsula liberally scattered with archaeological traces and marks of ancient settlements. It is now a Nature Reserve and from its height there is "a fantastic view which is unbelievably rich in imagery". Down by the shore there are soft cliffs whose powdery colours range from white and pale amethyst to strong ochre. A spit of sand and shingle runs out from

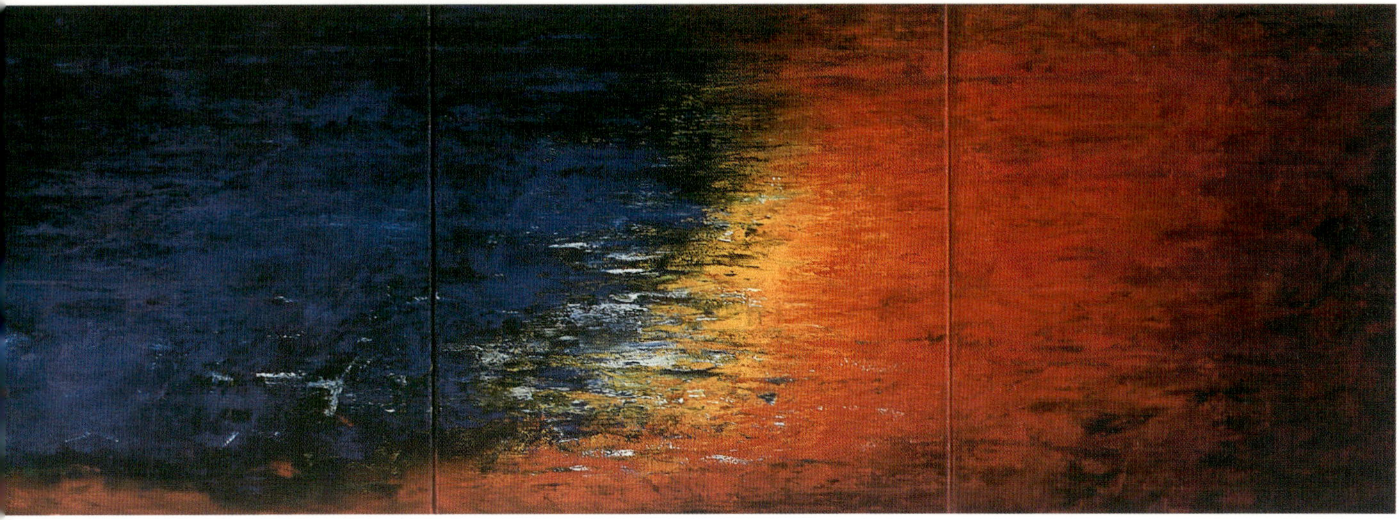

Night and Day Quartet (2000)

Hengistbury to form a natural southern breakwater for Christchurch Harbour. Brewster has made many landscape drawings of this stretch of coast. These are works which fall between the boundaries of figuration and abstraction.

Although primarily a painter, he has always given serious time to drawing. Drawing was strongly encouraged by Dennis Creffield who was initially his Tutor at Brighton. Creffield believed that drawing was a justifiable activity; with it came disciplined observation and new insight into a subject. Creffield's own strong charcoal drawings, which included a series of French and English cathedrals, became an inspiration for Brewster. "Creffield had a particular feeling for drawing and drawing from the motif. He ran a life studio with models each week, so I worked at drawing and painting from models, then going out and doing landscape work on my own."

Landscape drawing for Brewster has never been the recording of specifics, instead it has been a struggle to get down on paper a sense of the place and its fundamental structure, "trying to evoke something, something sensual, of what I feel about the place". Brewster's drawings are direct, emotional responses to a landscape which, like a roller-coaster, is never still. His drawings are always done on the spot and are specific to that place, to the atmosphere and weather at that time. Normally a drawing is completed in one go. "I find it very hard to go back to a drawing. They vary from little sketches which take a few minutes to the big charcoal drawings that might take the best part of a day. It uses a lot of energy and concentration ... a tremendous amount of time to really work a drawing, especially a heavy charcoal drawing. They're physically demanding, you can't do them all the time. Not every one works out, sometimes it gets lost, it just doesn't come right. They are done for their own sake. They are complete in themselves ... I'm not looking for drawing to get ideas for painting ... If the drawing doesn't have a power and emotion and evocation there's not much point in me doing it because I don't want a diagram of something, I want something living and working in and of itself."

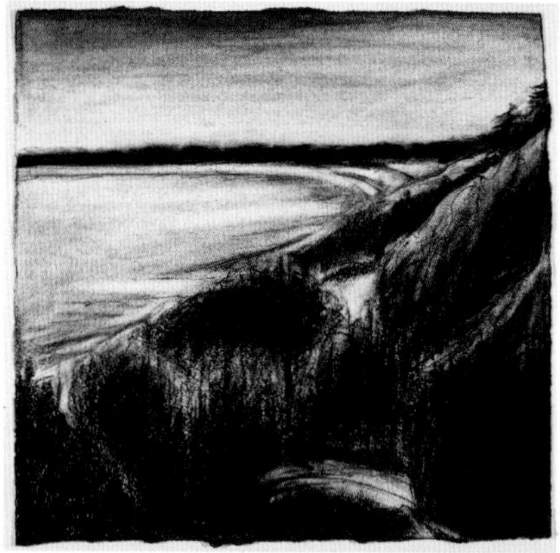

Dorset Coast Looking West (2000)

Brewster's drawings are not only of the local coastline but also of small woodlands, such as those along the River Stour. He also draws quintessentially English gardens and landscapes, working with both formal and non-formal gardens. He has drawn at Encombe, Upton and Kingston Lacey. In such places, he has not concentrated on grandeur, history or fine detail but has instead sought out abstract elements, such as "light falling across other forms, areas of dark and shade, things shifting ... ideas which are archetypal". Like Paul Nash, Brewster seeks out the spirit, the atmosphere of the place, and again like Nash, he can find it in familiar and tended areas. For Nash, early memories and experiences of Kensington Gardens and the family home at Iver Heath became places which were 'strangely beautiful and excitingly unsafe', where 'magic lay within itself, implicated in its own design'[3].

Although drawing is an activity that Brewster will always engage in, painting is his primary activity. As an art student of the Seventies, Brewster recalls the move away from painting to conceptual art, one popular practitioner then being Bruce McLean and his work with the camera. However, there were also exhibitions in London of painters such as Leon Kossof and Frank Auerbach, whose canvasses were covered with thick, heavy paint. Kossof and Auerbach, along with Creffield, were pupils of David Bomberg (1890-1957) who in his paintings of the 1920s and 30s used paint as a complete structural entity. Bomberg used loaded brushes, gesture and bodily weight as part of the medium.

Paint was given equal weight with the given object (Lynton, 1993)[4]. It was this way of handling paint, of building layers and constantly reworking surfaces that first attracted Brewster to Bomberg's work. While still at secondary school he began his own experimentation of using paint as thickly textured impasto.

During his subsequent Foundation Year at Hertfordshire College of Art and Design (1970-71), Brewster continued to work with "oil paint in quite a heavy way; a Soutine, Kokoschka, expressionist kind of way". Then, in the second year he began to move away from "a fairly broad painterly, expressionist approach to traditional subject matter into greater interest in abstraction and colour". He had become interested in the paintings of American Abstract Expressionists such as Willem de Kooning, Jackson Pollock and Mark Rothko. He liked their feeling for colour, their involvement with paint and scale. In particular, he admired Nicholas de Stael and Hans Hofmann as well as English painters such as Peter Lanyon and Ivon Hitchens. "These painters have, along with John Hoyland, Gillian Ayres, Howard Hodgkin and Bert Irvin, all contributed to a wonderful, rich Expressionist colour tradition which on the face of it doesn't seem to fit well with a perceived English monochrome tradition."

Nature Painting No. 116 (2000)

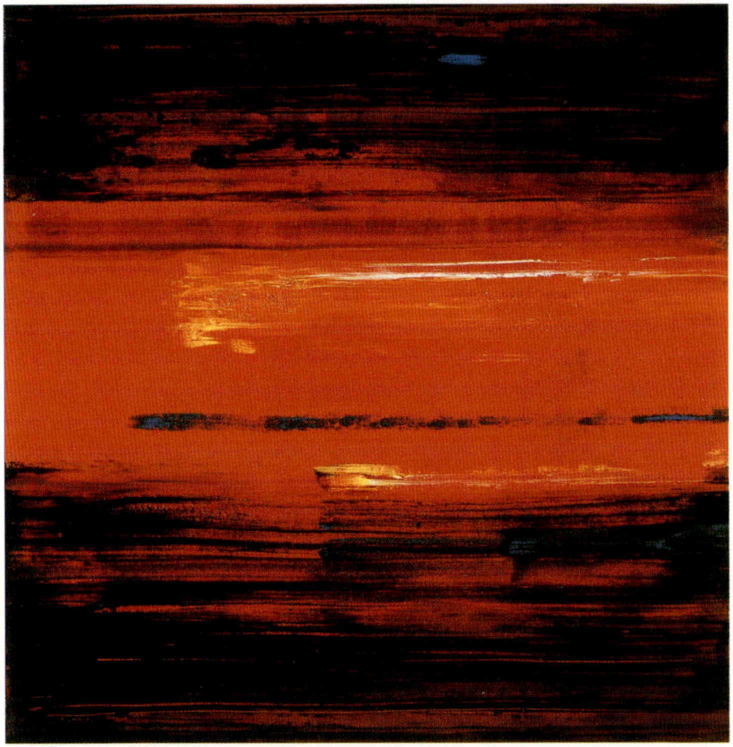

Since Brighton, Brewster's mode of working very directly with oil paint has continued: "The whole heart of me goes into making abstract, very lyrical colour paintings." These paintings, unlike his drawings, rarely make reference to specific locations. His present series of work mostly comes under the umbrella title of *Nature Paintings*. One recent painting belonging to this series is *Nature Painting 116, Headland series* (2000).

Brewster's painting is unashamedly dramatic and passionate in the tradition of Turner. It is also Romantic and lyrical, poetic and musical. He says: "I have doubted at stages when I've gone adrift a bit - the work has become slightly harder edged and perhaps more diagrammatic, geometric and so on. That area of abstraction, by and large, doesn't interest me at all; I find it unemotional, un-engaging, not such a sense of feeling.

I lose contact with it when it goes too far in that direction." Instead, he wishes to hold on to a form of painting that is "somehow suggestive, evocative and related to landscape, to land ideas and images. That aspect of work is always there, bouncing around, even when I get a little removed from it. I always come back to it."

In the 1980s, Brewster used pale colours in many of his impressionist water 'Monet Lake-side' paintings. There was a marked occurrence of greens, yellows and whites and the paintings often contained the word light in their title, such as *Winter Light Triptych* or *Shadows and Light*. There was a dreamlike element to them, a Romanticism which contrasted with a second series of "black and white work, of cliffs and waterfalls which related to the black and white quality in drawings".

When beginning a painting, Brewster prepares a canvas by painting some colour onto it, just thinly to begin with. It will be one of endless underpaintings because he usually knows, that at the very minimum, the canvas is going to be worked over half a dozen times or more. "It's the nature of the surface of the paint that I like to happen." For many years now, Brewster's dominant colours have been rich blues, reds and yellows. Why he chooses to work with the colours he does and not work with a tonal palette of earth colours is a question that he feels there is no answer to: "You almost don't want an answer, you don't want to work everything out."

For the last seven years he has painted on square canvasses. Before that, for ten or fifteen years, he worked with the more traditional landscape or portrait format but then the square surfaced with the *Beauty and Sadness* paintings and mono prints of 1996. Since then he has found that by restricting himself to a square format certain elements of composition are concentrated, in particular abstract qualities such as proportion, scale, colour reference, nature of the mark and the surface. He has also used square canvasses as building blocks, coloured units, assembling them, as in the *Night and Day* paintings, to become a diptych, triptych, quartet (as in *Night and Day Quartet,* 2000) or polyptych. These poly-works are oriented to an horizontal axis but he has also experimented with placing them in the vertical axis. The larger of Brewster's canvasses can be up to two metres square while the smaller ones are about half a metre square.

Brewster nearly always uses the medium of oil, although for his silk-screen prints he uses acrylic. "There are qualities in acrylic you can't get in oils, certain ways of glazing and layering which bring out other intensities which I love." Brewster originally learned the technique of silk-screen printing at a postgraduate course run by Harvey Daniel at Brighton. Later, between 1994 and 1997, he was offered a series of residences at Lowick House Print Workshop which resulted in a new collection of prints. Many of these prints celebrate the joy of colour but those of the *Beauty and Sadness* series have an introspective darkness, a literal blackness which speaks of fragile emotion and possible threat. In the Jill George Gallery Exhibition of 1997 many of these prints were included alongside paintings bearing the same title. In the paintings large areas of black paint shut out other colours and dominate as a pushing, powerful force. However, black never fully triumphs, and the other colours never completely submit. The paintings determinedly reach forward and remain a fighting part of life. Brewster's most recent print series is titled *Heartsong* (*Heartsong 177,* 2001).

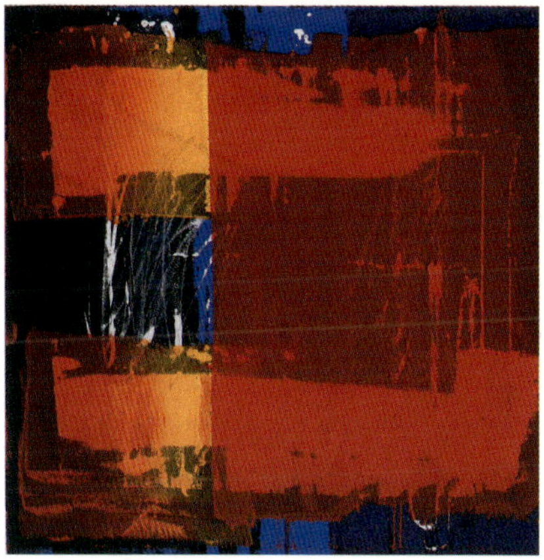

Heartsong No.177 (2001)

Following his last Lowick residency Brewster abandoned the domination of black and returned to a broader palette. He developed a series of *Night Music* paintings. ''Nearly all the images have the presence of a vibrant ultramarine blue that glowed in the studio when the light faded from the landscape around, and danced to the music I played as I worked - singing colours like stained glass' (Brewster, 1998)[5]. If Brewster had to be identified with any one colour it would be blue: "blue to white and everything in between. There is something about blue, the whole spectrum of blues that I've always been totally caught up in and find very difficult to get away from." For him, blues are an evocation of mood and atmosphere. He can lift a blue to the cold glassy light of early morning or drop it into the deep shadows of night. He can celebrate its shimmer and sparkle or bury it in the dark depths of a storm.

For Brewster, colour will always be the central force of his work: its emotion, lyricism and power. Starting from a love of blue, Brewster then reached out to the dyad partner of red. This red/blue dyad has over the years become a constant theme and been central to both the *Night Music* and *Nature* paintings. In the polyptychs of *Night and Day,* red and blue meet in a furnace glow of yellow, orange, white and green, the colours of mid-day sun and of creation. Beyond them is complete darkness, an infinite cosmos of burnt sienna and black. These paintings are not only about the hours of a day but about the whole gamut of time. They become an adventure, a connective thread to the wider scene and drama of T.S.Eliot's 'time present, time past .... and time future contained in time past'.[6]

Though Brewster works within the more formal considerations of abstraction, it is the flux of 'real' nature, its dynamic change and restlessness, its structures and forms that continue to stimulate and inspire him. His is always an emotional response to the world out there, to walks along cliffs, to a brilliant sunset or a heavy winter's day. He acknowledges that, as a painter, "I could perfectly well live somewhere else besides Dorset, find some place that is similarly stimulating but that isn't the point. The point is, I have found it a wonderful, inspiring place to live." Being able to observe at first hand events such as the play of light on water or moving shadows across a cliff face is important. It reinforces for Brewster the wonder of nature, which is neither controlled nor constant.

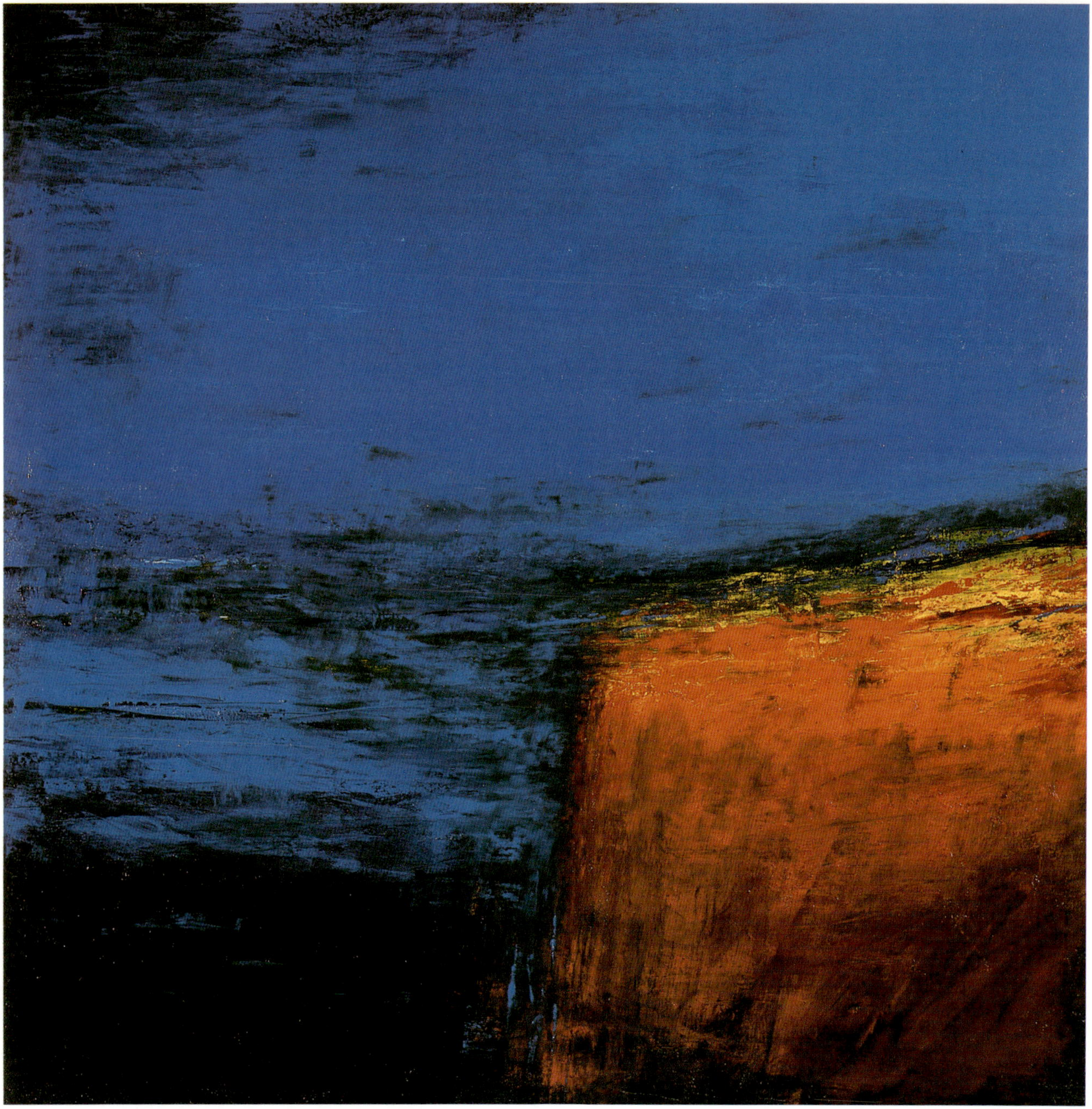

Nature Painting No. 100, Headland series (2000)

Biography

1952 Born Oxford
1970-71 Hertforshire College of Art and Design
1971-74 Brighton Polytechnic, Fine Art BA (Hons.)
1974-75 Brighton Polytechnic, Post-Graduate Printmaking
1977 Eastern Arts Award
1980-89 Lecturer, East Arts College
Visiting Lecturer, Winchester School of Art
1989 - Lecturer, Arts Institute, Bournemouth
1990 Moved to Dorset
1991 British Council Award to exhibit in USA
1992 Arts Award, Bournemouth Borough Council
1994 Openshaw Printmaking Award, Lowick House, Cumbria
1995 Arts Council of England, Development Award
1996/97 Printmaking Residency, Lowick House, Cumbria
1997 Monograph to accompany Retrospective exhibition
1999 Research and Scholarship Award, Arts Institute, Bournemouth

Collections include

Sainsburys plc
Scandia Life
Poole Museum, Dorset
Pallant House, West Sussex
Dell Computers, Limerick
Dublin Institute of Technology
Central Japan Railway Company
Winchester Health Authority
BMW (UK)
Schroder Investment, London
First Interstate Bank of California
Midland Bank plc
Lloyds TSB
IBM (UK) Ltd
St. Thomas's Hospital
The Economist
Unilever, plc
Ashmoleum Museum, Oxford
British Museum, London
Russell Cotes Art Gallery & Museum
Cable & Wireless plc
The Open University
Arts Institute, Bournemouth
London Business School

Martyn Brewster's work is also in many private collections in Great Britain, Holland, Germany, USA and Australia

Selected solo exhibitions

1977 Hertfordshire College of Art (two person)
1978 Christy's Art Gallery, Brighton
1982 Harlow Playhouse Gallery, Essex
Hornsey Library Gallery, London
1983 Peterborough City & Art gallery
Letchworth Museum & Art Gallery
1984 Bury St. Edmunds Art Gallery, Suffolk
London College of Furniture
1985 Brighton Polytechnic (two person)
Wilmer Cutler & Pickering Law Associates
1986 Warwick Arts Trust, London
Winchester Gallery (touring exhibition)
1987 Woodlands Gallery, London
1988 *Shadows and Light,* Thumb Gallery
Bede Gallery, Jarrow
1989 Thumb Gallery (two person)
1990 *Light Fall,* Thumb Gallery, London
Atlanta '91, Atlanta USA (Jill George)
1992-01 Jill George Gallery, London (ten exhibitions)
1993 Upstairs Gallery, Upton Country Park
Pallant House Gallery, West Sussex
Russell-Cotes Art Gallery and Museum
1993-00 On Line Gallery, Southampton (four exhibitions)
1994 Dorset County Museum, Dorchester
Russell-Cotes Art Gallery and Museum
Quay Arts Centre, Isle of Wight
Pallant House Gallery, West Sussex
Brighton Museum & Art Gallery
Arts Institute, Bournemouth
Atrium Gallery, Bournemouth University
2001 Royal West of England Academy
Link Gallery, King Alfred's College, Winchester

Numerous Selected Group Exhibitions 1986-2001
Most Recent

2000 San Francisco Art Fair (Jill George Gallery)
Toronto Art Fair (Jill George Gallery)
20th Century Art Fair (Jill George Gallery)
'2K,2K' Jill George Gallery
Bournemouth University
2001 Art 2001, London
On Line Gallery, Southampton
Bournemouth University, Dorset
Edwin Day Gallery, Toronto

Main Literature

Simon Olding *Martyn Brewster*, Scholar Press (1997)

GEORGE DANNATT

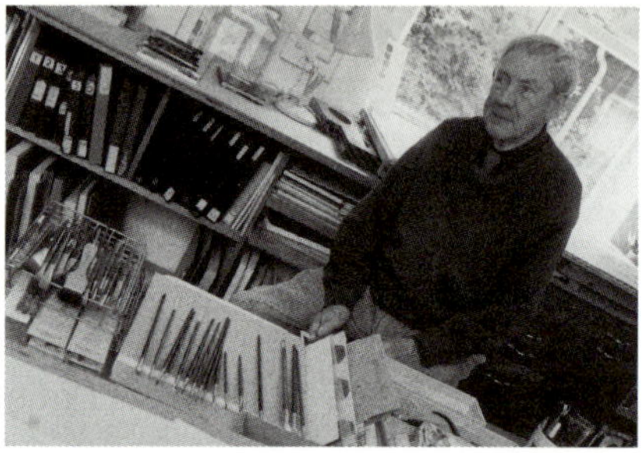

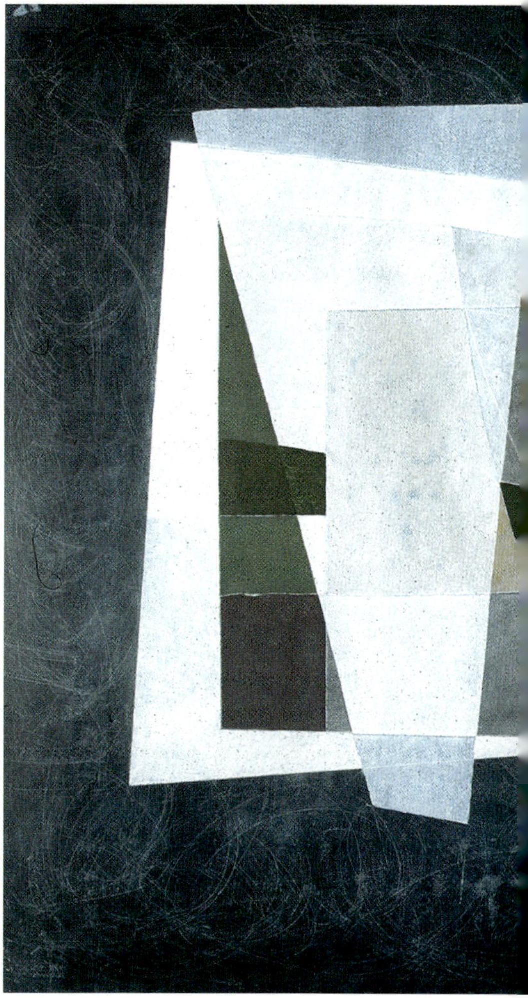

Encountering George and Ann Dannatt's house and George's studio is a stimulating experience, something akin to that obtained from encountering Jim Ede's Kettle's Yard in Cambridge. The house and studio are separate buildings set within a lightly wooded area: in February there are catkins of copsed hazel, dark, glossed ivy and large areas of very white snowdrops. The house has a feeling of warmth and quietness together with an atmosphere of humour, enthusiasm and activity. The interior is pervasively white with a great number of shelves packed with books, music and orchestral scores; there are specialised books on music, painting and literature in both English and other languages. Alterations and additions to the original stone cottage have been made over the years and in the largest room - very much a work room - two grand pianos offer contrasting timbres and keyboard 'touch' for daily practice. A full range of recording and amplifying equipment provide exceptional opportunities for music listening. There is no television.

Uninterrupted light through the windows reveals a fine collection of paintings, prints, reliefs and sculptures. There is a representative body of Dannatt's own work, much work by painters and sculptors of the West Penwith post-war era along with work by other painters who have strong and significant connections with the continental Constructivist tradition.

The Dannatts have a zest for life, art, music, literature - and people, though they live within this somewhat isolated house and surroundings. What brought them to Wessex was their intense interest in the work of Thomas Hardy. Through frequent visits to Dorchester they became deeply involved in the land and history of Dorset and Wiltshire. Thus, they explored these revealing landscapes, frequently following the scenes of Hardy's novels and poems, but with no car and very restricted bus services in the early years after the War. There was an increasing desire to move to Dorset, but Dannatt's professional work was in London. They overcame the travelling problem by finding a cottage in the Vale of Wardour, within a two hour train journey of London. This they used for occasional holidays or weekends, but eventually the cottage became the core for the creation of a bigger and permanent home.

For some forty years now, the Wessex scene has been a formative element in Dannatt's work, work basically abstract but often derived from aspects of texture, form, rhythm and colour found in ancient landscapes. Within much of his work Dannatt manages to create dynamic tension and movement, with a sensitive selection and interrelation of colours, colours forcefully strong, or condensed and restrained as in *Veiled Landscape - Dole's Ash* (2000).

George Dannatt was brought up in an artistically-oriented home and was early made aware of classical painting through his parents' and grandparents' choice of works, many in good reproductions; and through lantern slides. In fact: "the type of restricted visual education of those days". Similarly, in music there was the 'His Master's Voice' wind-up gramophone, a fair selection of records and. most importantly, the piano. It was through these latter sources that his over-riding interest in music was aroused, with the result that he was given for his fifteenth birthday, 16th August, 1932, a ticket for his first Henry Wood Promenade Concert: "A pretty stiff concert but exciting, for it included the first performance of Ravel's Pianoforte Concerto with the incisive music of Paul Hindemith."

Veiled Landscape - Dole's Ash (2000)

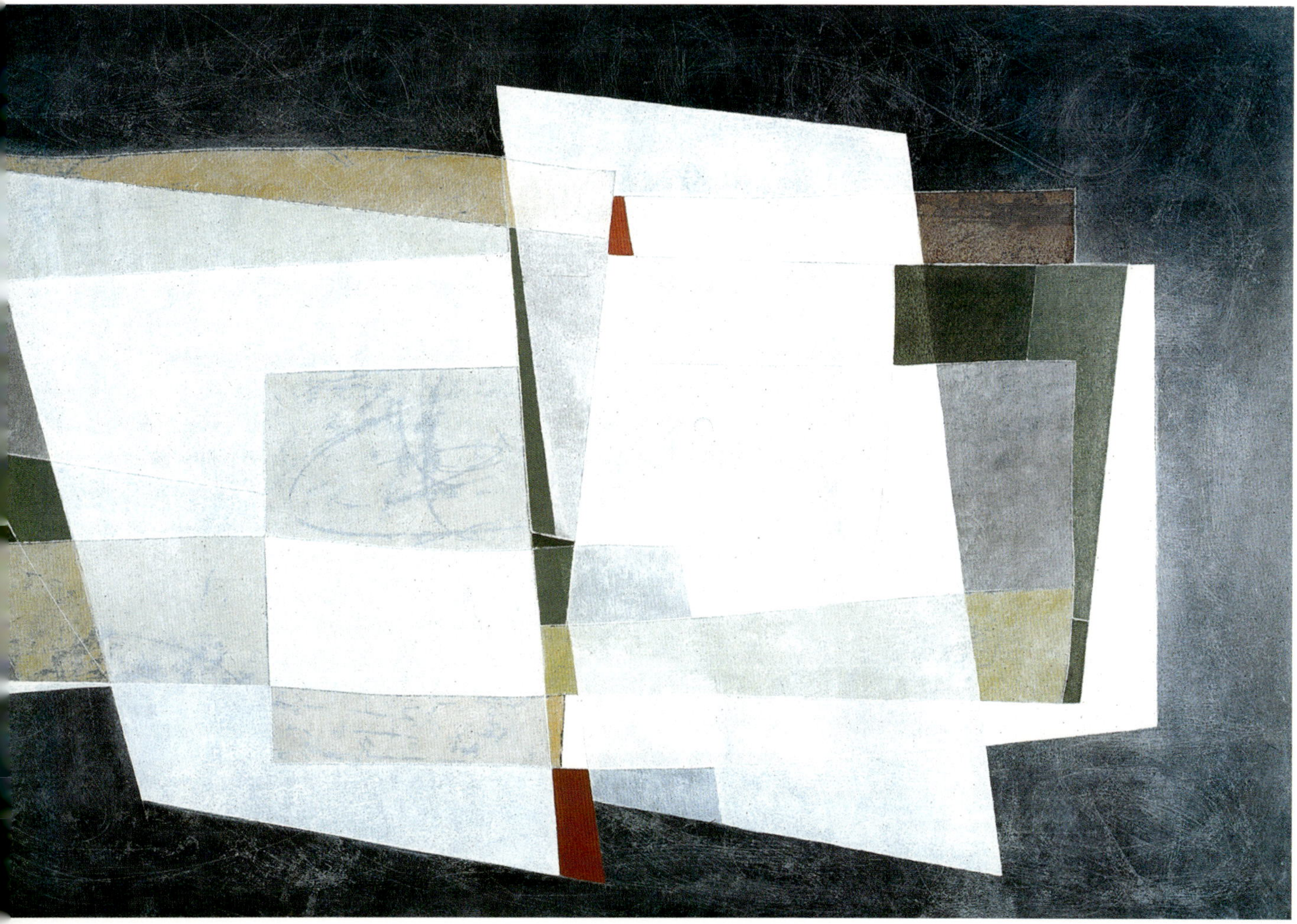

Dannatt enjoyed little at school, detested regimentation and refused to take part in organised games. However, through the influence of a 'remarkable' English master, he developed a keen interest in Literature and languages. His preference in those early days was to be in his timber workshop which he designed and built himself at the age of fourteen. "My passion was to make a radio controlled boat. At that time, many people who lived in Blackheath regularly went down to Greenwich Reach to see the huge liners coming up into the docks, towed by two or three tugs; the shape of the boats and their movement through the water was most evocative". This interest in boats (and he built several models) was later reinforced when he started going to Cornwall in the Sixties. A series of five Newlyn Quay Drawings (1960) are based upon the shapes of the discarded metal cut in the quay boat-repair workshops - shapes sketched or photographed - an oblique way of thinking and working indicative of a painter who often sees and selects the less obvious on which to construct.

In 1940 Dannatt qualified as a Chartered Surveyor (elected FRICS in 1957) but was almost immediately conscripted into the Army, in which he remained for four years before being invalided out in March 1944. After some months of recuperation, which gave him a good opportunity to resume his music studies, he rejoined the family business. At the same time, he began writing music reviews for Ralph Hill, who was the Radio Times Music Editor and Music Critic on the Daily Mail. Soon after this, he became a music critic on the London News Chronicle, a position which he held for twelve years, in addition to his daily office work. "I was in on all the resurgence of Covent Garden, the many concerts, ballets and so on. Then the job packed up, as did the Chronicle two or three years later. I had been working on concerts, opera and ballet for anything up to four nights a week for twelve years and I was at a loss when I found myself at home every night. So I started seriously to paint. We lived conveniently for Cork Street and were frequently at the galleries. The first recognition of the sort of paintings that I liked was through these galleries, particularly Waddington, who showed Wells, Hilton, McKenzie, Mitchell and many other artists of the St. Ives West Penwith school."

Dannatt was attracted to the Constructivism of Gabo, Hepworth and Nicholson, artists who had a strong interest in seeking out and making use of geometric forms found within 'lyrical' landscapes. These artists also drew inspiration from the science and mathematics of their day. They used theoretical models as new visual stimuli to develop fresh ways of thinking and working. Thus, for example, Gabo explored new materials in his 3D constructions; Hepworth did a whole series of crystal drawings; and Nicholson explored the circle against the flat plane. It was interest in such work that took the Dannatts for many years to that area of Cornwall, which not only housed a number of the artists whose work Dannatt so greatly admired, but also provided that 'emotive scene' which so clearly influenced their work. "The first time we went to Cornwall, Ann and I had the stimulating experience of staying with Delia and Patrick Heron at their uniquely-situated home, Eagle's Nest. It was exhilarating to be taken to explore that area with Patrick, especially on a day when a sea fog set in and the granite and air sparkled with the special light closely associated with that mythical area between the two seas. On innumerable later visits we stayed at Penzance and that re-inforced our friendship with John Wells and Denis Mitchell. I suppose that my biggest influence was through Gabo, Nicholson and Hepworth as filtered through their influence upon Wells and Mitchell." Both Wells and Mitchell became close personal friends.

With another painting colleague of the St. Ives area, Roy Conn, Dannatt learnt of Malevich and the Russian School of Suprematism. The Suprematists replaced identifiable brush marks with anonymous monotone surfaces, free lines with ruled lines, and complexity with apparent geometric simplicity. For someone such as Dannatt, who felt drawn by the lyricism of landscape, to favour a more exact kind of painting may seem surprising. However, perhaps stemming from his professional career as a surveyor, Dannatt seems always to have had an inherent feeling for this way of working: "I think it came about partly because when I had finished a painting, I analysed it to myself and found so many points of contact, geometric contact, when I related the basic images to each other - a feeling for form which one finds on, say, analysing a Mozart Sonata."

In comparison to the majority of painters Dannatt came relatively late to painting and he postponed exhibiting any of his work for many years. He first showed at Penwith Gallery, due to the encouragement of the St. Ives painter, Breon O'Casey. O'Casey visited the Dannatts in Central London. "He is a very quiet Irishman and as he sat in my music room after a long time of looking around, he said: 'Who are all these paintings by?' and I said, 'They're mine.' Another long pause and he said, 'Do you show your work?' I said, 'No, I just paint for myself'. 'Oh', he said: 'You ought to, you know. I can introduce you to the Penwith Gallery and you could show there'. So I started sending work to Penwith Gallery and I came to show there regularly for some twelve to fifteen years - and also, of course at the Newlyn Gallery, where I had an important retrospective exhibition in 1981."

Post and Dune (1994)

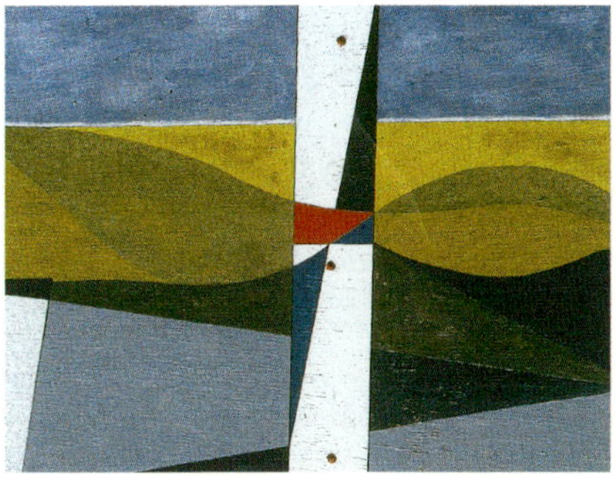

Dannatt's notebooks contain both drawings and written notes, which he uses when preparing his work in the studio. He never paints in the open air. He is also a keen photographer, having initially been taught various photographic techniques by his father. Using differential focusing, (that is focussing on a nearby object and letting the rest go out of focus), helps him find a way into many of his paintings, one example being *Post and Dune* (1994).

Chesil Bank and Portland are favourite locations: "It is the Portland stone that intrigues me, the whiteness, the texture, the tactile surfaces ... the many cuttings out. I also think the sight of Portland from Ringstead Cliff is one of the most evocative I know." Many of

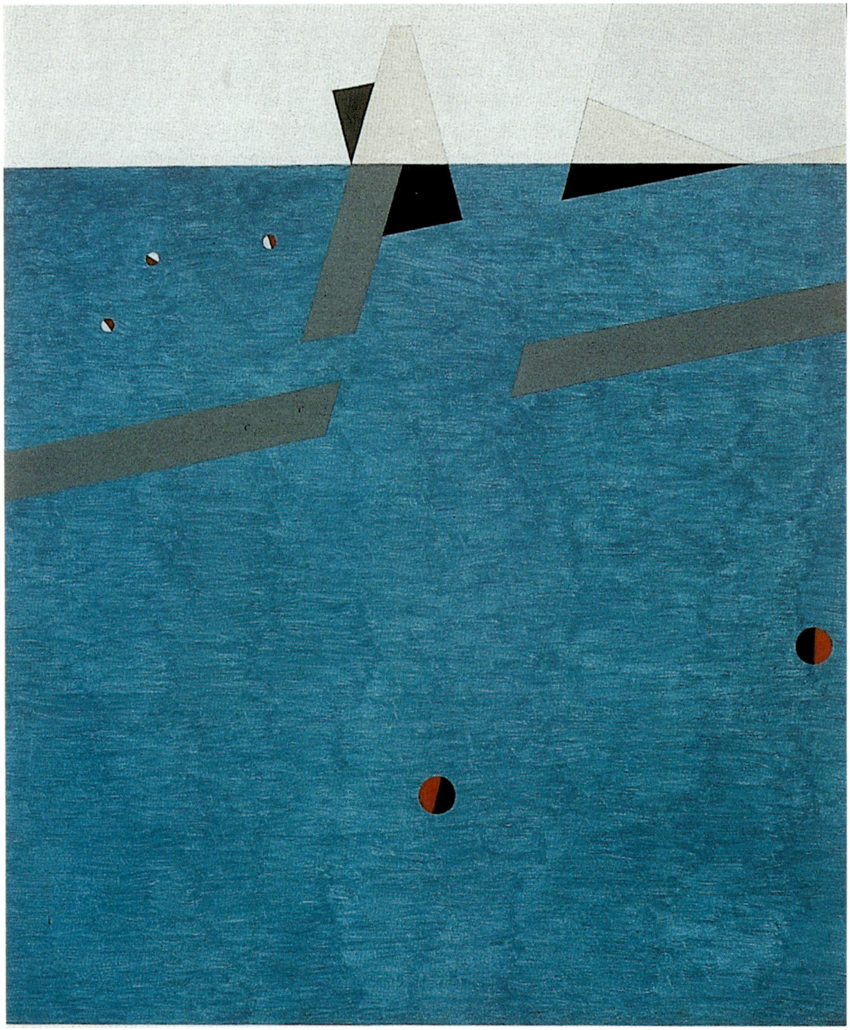

Portland (1989)

Dannatt's Portland paintings, such as *Portland* (1989), and *Portland* (1950), are derived from this Ringstead perspective. In these paintings, you see a vast expanse of sea, far harbour walls and floats left by fishermen. Dannatt worked for a period of four to five years before completing the paintings to his satisfaction.

Although Dannatt now generally paints in oil, he restricted himself to gouache for several years, which was, he believes, a good painting apprenticeship. He will still sometimes use gouache now to provide a textural contrast within a basically oil painting.

As regards colour, Dannatt, like many painters, 'feels it' through an instinctive sense and relates it to the subject in hand. "So I can remember, I record the mixes on a card to which I can refer, which is particularly important if I want to alter the painting and have to mix a colour up again... Also when I'm creating another painting I make use of these colour cards in trying them against the new painting. But this means I have a permanent reference system". Dannatt rarely uses paint straight from the tube; just occasionally when he seeks a strong accentuation point. Quite frequently an accent of red can be found. "When you're walking in the country there's nearly always a bit of red somewhere, either a flower or a shed or a piece of machinery."

Dannatt's paintings invariably begin as a sketch or note, as in *Bazon Hill Figuration* (1999). This painting was "based on a hill that you see when you drive to Dorchester on the top road, looking over towards Cerne Abbas". From a sketch Dannatt makes a drawing and prepares a painted support, usually of wood or softboard, before transferring the drawing. He creates both flat and textured surfaces. Textures are achieved by incising with etching tools or by scratching the surfaces with sandpaper or a razor blade. Very rarely are any brush marks visible as he uses flat and square sable brushes, and small ones at that, even for large paintings. Sometimes he incorporates collage material such as painted Japanese papers or thin lead foil. He uses a wide variety of supports which he feels very much add to the individuality of his work - supports include 'marouflage' - linen glued to board, the board itself having its own quality, as when salvaged driftwood is used. "A variety of both soft and hardboards are used, Japanese 'textured' paper on card: the possibilities are endless."

Blue Channel (1999)

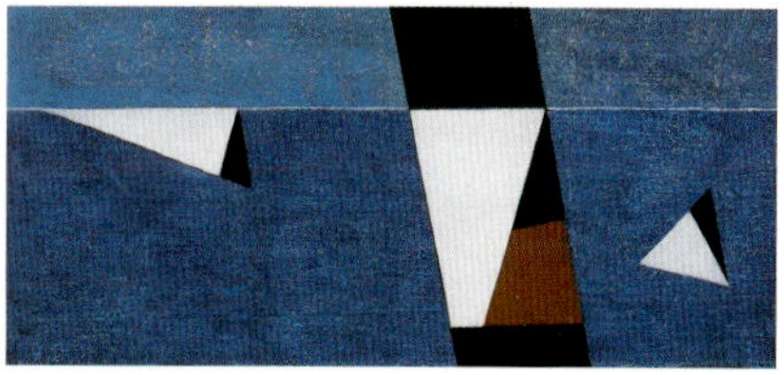

Dannatt does not believe that his colour selection has changed much over the years, except more recently he has become "a bit obsessed by black". A favourite colour is probably a blackish green. Blue is another favoured colour. *Blue Channel* (1999) was created using two variations of blue while *Composition in Blue on Slate Grey* (1997), makes use of four blues - cobalt, manganese, sèvre and Prussian blue - all of which are in 'counterpoint' with each other.

Detail *Blue Channel* (1999)

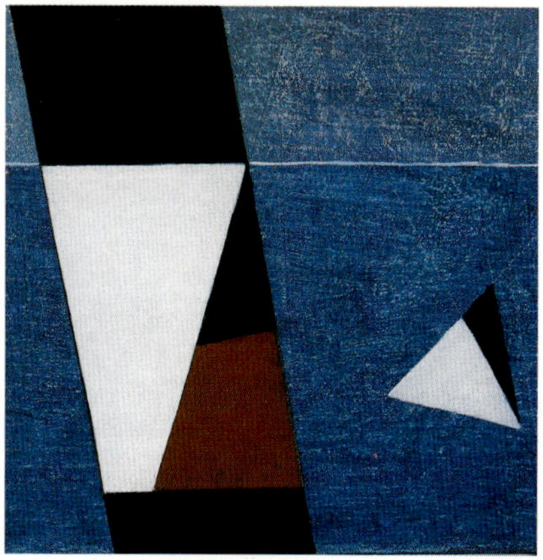

Dannatt feels a sensitivity to places that 'are evoked by pre-history, to the country around Dorchester (*Poundbury Landscape*,1997) to Maiden Castle and the ancient burial mounds known in Dorset as 'tumps'. Sometimes, after a walk, he will make a graphite drawing in 'wobbly thick lines' of hill shapes, strip lynchets or ancient field boundaries. He is interested in the aerial aspect of them: "you see from the air what is implied by walking on the ground". He is always especially happy when he finds a circle or quasi circle within a landscape.

With his painting Dannatt "hopes to convey a musicality, something of that emotion which you get when listening to a poem or piece of music. It's inside you; it comes out."

The relationship of painting to music is a subject close to his heart but, as he says, it is extremely difficult to pin down. "I think one notices painting in music rather than the other way round. When you're playing a Mozart Sonata ... you discover a pattern, a structure which is not so clearly apparent in a performance of the whole piece. It is the overall impression, rather than the detail, which is conveyed, yet the whole cannot exist without the underlying structure. So with my painting." For Dannatt his work is a continual quest. "The quest is endless and raises eternal self-questioning. Is this work truly satisfactory? Have I achieved what I was aiming for?" Such questions continue to bite at the heels of George Dannatt and no doubt will always continue to do so.

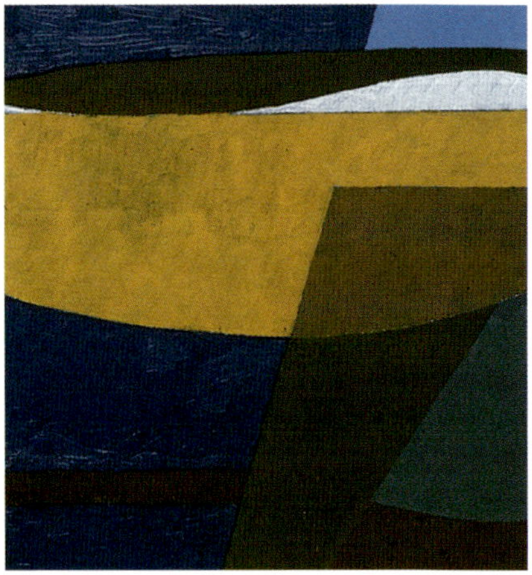

Detail

Poundbury Landscape (1997)

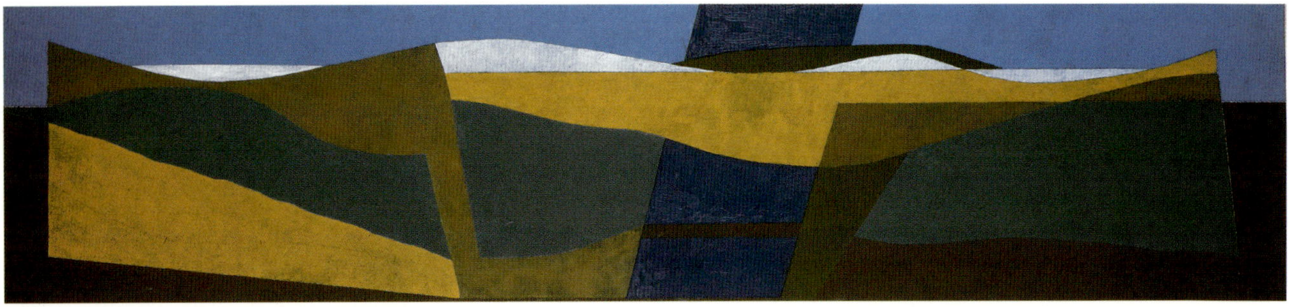

Biography

1915	Born Blackheath, London
1940	Qualified as Chartered Surveyor (FRICS)
1940–1944	Army Service
1943	Married Ann Doncaster
1944	Rejoined family business as Chartered Surveyor
1945-1956	Music critic for *News Chronicle* and *Penguin Music Magazine,* periodicals, programme notes, record and CD sleeves
1948	Elected Member of Critics' Circle, Music Section (now Honorary member)
	First of regular visits to Dorset
1956	Became a free-lance music critic
1958	Bought a house on the Dorset-Wiltshire border
1969	Retired from Chartered Surveying
	Painting and music became full time career
1970	Associate member: Penwith Society of Artists
1973	First showed at Newlyn Society of Artists (subsequently elected full member)
1974	Member of the Garrick Club
1980	Wrote 'Introduction: Arthur Bliss 1891-1975' for Novello publication (one of many writings about the composer)
1981	Member of the Savage Club
1986	Established a Charitable Trust for the advancement of education in the visual arts

Solo Exhibitions

1980	Galerie Schreiner, Basel, Switzerland
1981	Newlyn-Orion Retrospective (1960-1981)
1984	Galerie Artica, Cuxhaven, Germany
1988	Michael Parkin Gallery, London
1990	Galerie Artica, Cuxhaven on occasion of publication of book: One Way of Seeing
1992	New Ashgate Gallery, Farnham
1993	Dorset County Museum, Dorchester
1994	Chesil Gallery, Portland, Dorset
1995	*Structural Harmonies* The Book Gallery, St. Ives
1997	*Sonorities* The Town Mill Gallery, Lyme Regis, Dorset
1997	*Quest and Bequest* Dorset County Museum
1997	*Structural Syntax* The Book Gallery, St. Ives
1997	*Lines of Seeing* Russell-Cotes Art Gallery, Bournemouth
2000	*Themes & Variations* Maltby Contemporary Art, Winchester

Selected Group Shows

1970	Penwith Gallery, St. Ives
	(Contributed to a further fifteen exhibitions)
1974-2001	Newlyn Art Gallery (many exhibitions)
1975	Orion Gallery, Penzance (Three man show with John Wells and Alexander MacKenzie)
1978	Newlyn Society of Artists, Pont Aven, Brittany
1981	Kunst aus Cornwall, Galerie Artica, Cuxhaven
1983/90	Michael Parkin Gallery, London
	Bath Art Fair (Michael Parkin Gallery)
	Chicago Art Fair (Michael Parkin Gallery)
1987	Galerie Artica, Cuxhaven, 20th Anniversary Exhibition
1987/89	Andrew Jones Art, touring exhibition, London
1990	Redfern Gallery, London (two exhibitions)
1994	'Three Painters' Reed's Wharf Gallery, London
1997/98	Basel Art Fair, New Art Centre
1999	Newlyn Revisited: Wells, Mackenzie and Dannatt Broad Street Gallery, Lyme Regis, Dorset
2001	Festival Show (three person)
	Maltby Contemporary Art, Winchester

Collections

Galerie Artica, Cuxhaven, Germany

Stadt Bibliotek, Cuxhaven, Germany

R.A.F. Museum, Hendon

Russell Cotes Gallery & Museum, Bournemouth

Dorset County Museum, Dorchester

Cambridge University Library

Publications are many and various. They include

'One Way of Seeing' (1990), Hobnob Press & Galerie Artica, Cuxhaven

'Three essays' (1997) Simon Olding, Mark Bills and George Dannatt

VANESSA GARDINER

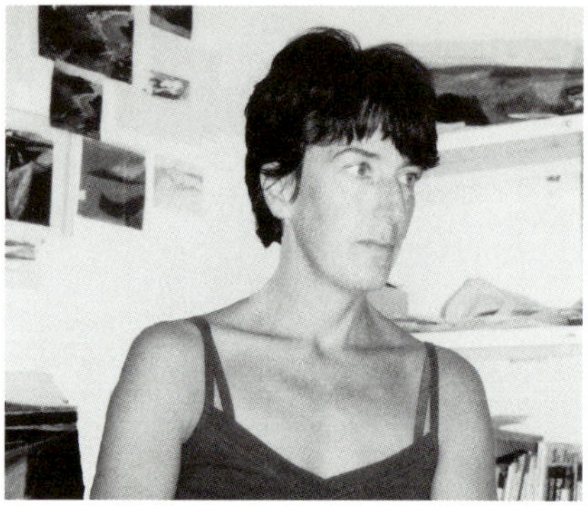

From Charmouth, the road climbs steeply west towards Lyme Regis. On this stretch of road, well hidden behind a high, verdant hedge, is Vanessa Gardiner's home and studio. A garden path edged with rosemary leads to the front door. The house was once the holiday home of her parents and before that of two Great Aunts with whom she used to stay for two or three-week periods every summer. Her first memories of the landscape stem from early morning walks along the cliffs just beyond Charmouth. In family groups they would walk the ancient track of Stonebarrow Hill, from where there are sweeping views to Start Point and Golden Cap. The Dorset coast is a coast of many-coloured cliffs, but the highest and most glowing of all is Golden Cap. This cliff stands a hundred and ninety one metres high and is a weighty mass of scarped sandstone topped by a plateau of greensand.

From her garden, Gardiner has a distant view of Charmouth and the sea, but closer by lies Conegar Hill, whose well defined shape, as painted in *November Landscape* (1992), rises amid an expansive framework of rolling countryside. Here, in this well tempered part of Dorset, the wider landscape comfortably accommodates miniature, self-contained scapes. They are reminiscent of the 'view-through scenes' painted behind many an Italian Renaissance Madonna and Child. Topographic links and similarities can be made between neat, outlined conical hills; delicately-traced trees and woods; deep diving valleys and exposed cliffs and paths.

November Landscape (1992)

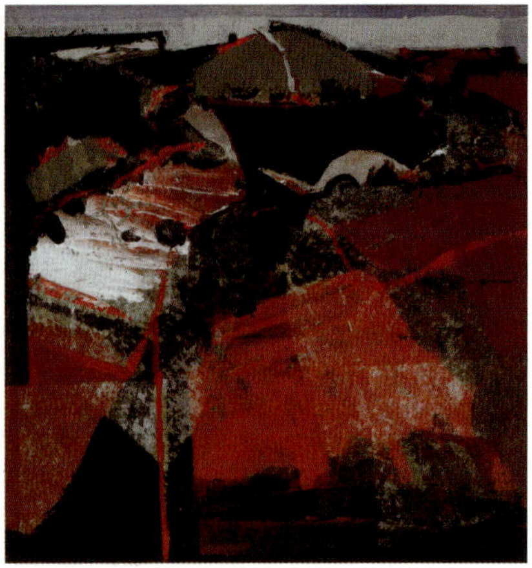

Gardiner's father was a Thomas Hardy enthusiast. It was this Hardy attachment which led to many family holidays either in Dorset, or in North Cornwall. In a sense, Gardiner reflects, she has been painting places for the last ten years which go right back to these very early times and experiences. Choosing to paint the landscapes she does has been both a conscious and subconscious affair: "I don't think you are aware of why it is you refer to things from your past, although, naturally it does have an emotional dimension to it."

Well before Hardy began to write his Wessex novels, Jane Austen had discovered Charmouth's 'retired bay' and 'dark cliffs'.[7] This stretch of coast can be a dangerous place, where sea cliffs such as Black Ven continue to collapse in slumping landslides.

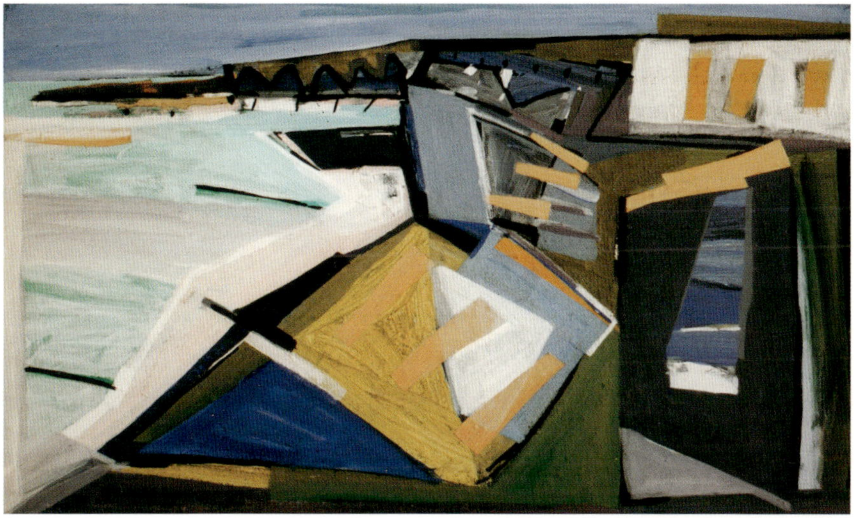

From Black Ven (1990)

Gardiner recalls that there used to be a road from Lyme to Charmouth but it 'disappeared' about 1965. Since then, there have been further cliff falls and landslips. The cause is a layer of blue lias, which, being quite impervious to water, encourages other strata to slip. This continual erosion leaves a forlorn, lonely place of tumbledown cliffs which Francis Bickley in 1911 likened to 'the brick-heaps of Titan builders'.[8]

In the early Nineties, Gardiner worked for about four years at Black Ven. She produced large oil paintings which for the most part related in colour to the landscape. She also completed smaller work in acrylic, to which she added collage material such as various papers and fragments of slate. It was the drama of Black Ven, its threatening instability, its continual state of flux and metamorphosis that captured her imagination. These paintings are strong but discordant, reflecting a true sense of the place. In this cliff series Gardiner worked in a fairly classic manner, a disciplined approach which continues in her work today.

In paintings, such as *From Black Ven* (1990) and *Rockfalls* (1990) formal considerations such as structure, form and line dominate. However, these paintings are also highly-charged works of emotion. One can sense the inescapable power of the situation as sections of cliff slip downwards to the sea, breaking away from the land on top of the cliff, while all around rocks crash and gather momentum, charging down and spilling without compunction on to sands below. Combining all this with a racing sea, there is a general air of exhilaration at the turn of events. Back from the cliff edge, fractured land is already shifting and re-formulating into new structural planes. Although it seems that 'the centre cannot hold', that all is impending slippery chaos, there remains a note of optimism: the land is re-inventing itself. These are dramatic paintings.

Although there is much abstraction in the Black Ven paintings, defining elements of the figurative are retained: there is horizon, distance, perspective and depth. They have a certain kinship to Peter Lanyon's high places and edges; of landscapes seen from the air. However, more than Lanyon, Gardiner finds it hard to completely abstract. She is continually searching for a way to produce an abstract picture which is still about place. In one way she says it is her biggest dilemma: "If it still feels like the place, I'm alright. If it starts to get more abstract then I can't justify it in my mind." Gardiner feels happier when she can 'read' the painting, relate it to a place.

Besides coastal landslips in Dorset, Gardiner has also drawn and painted several inland sites. In graphite she has drawn the land broadly sweeping and rising to the summit of Connegar Hill. It is a landscape of sharply-defined fields banded by tight hedges, narrow lanes, lone houses and dark clusters of trees. The horizon is high and the sea a distant line. In both drawing and painting, Gardiner's preferred perspective is from above, looking down. She likes the whole idea of having an aerial view of a scene. She has drawn from many high places around her home, such as Chilcombe and Chideock and also Eggardon Hill, a high, bare and lonely Iron Age site near Powerstock, built with a steep three-bank defence. Gardiner particularly liked the glimpses of the sea she could catch through the trees in the distance. *Eggardon Hill* was painted in 1992.

Drawing is the means by which Gardiner finds her way into any new subject; it is an integral part of the way she works. While at the Central School of Art and Design (1979-1982), drawing became a conscious, reflective part of her work. Her Tutor, David Haughton, taught Gardiner about staying with a drawing for more than the "allotted half an hour". Now when Gardiner is out in the landscape, the first half hour is spent just looking and drawing, trying to basically "get it right ... then, after about an hour, it's as if something else starts flowing through; it can take two or three hours ... it's that staying a bit longer. The activity of drawing will create shapes; new shapes that you might not have known were there before and which you can then build into your paintings."

Drawing gives Gardiner an architectural structure with which to work. It is also through selective, representational drawing that Gardiner uncovers paths of originality and

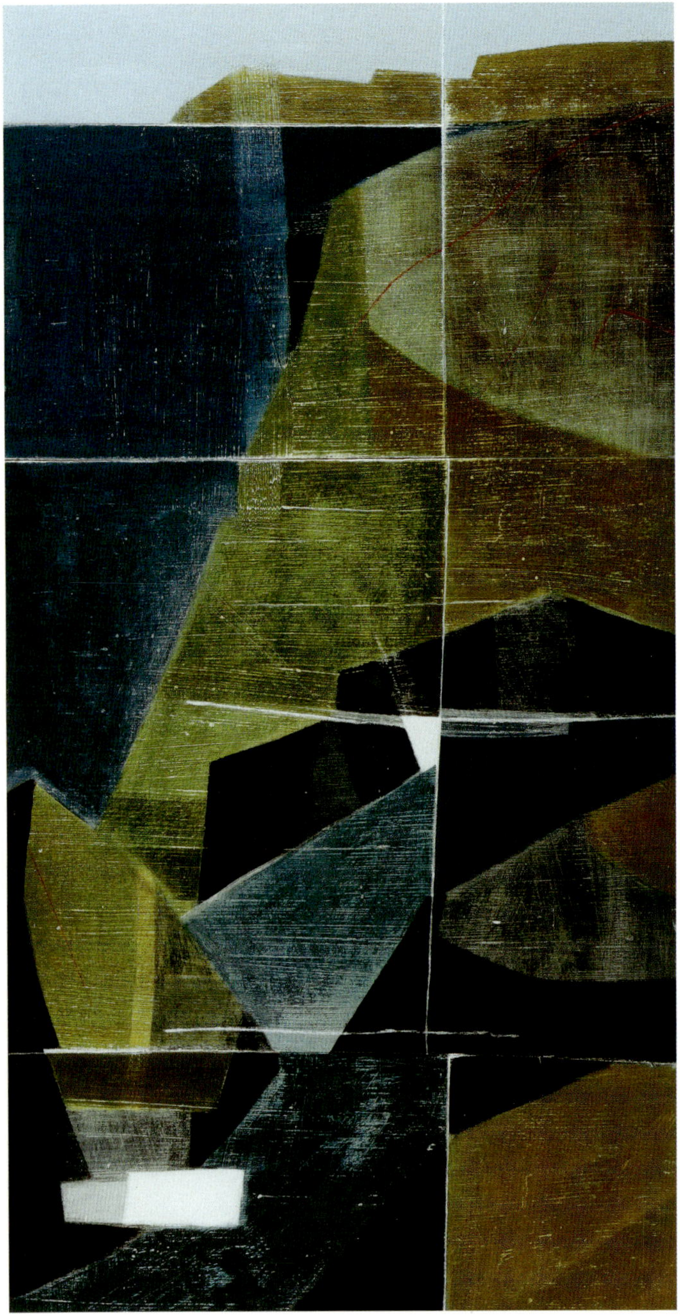

Vertical Landscape No.2 (2000)

invention. Once, when using a very small sketchbook, she found that the landscape would not fit on one page so she folded over the pages until she had used six pages. She then cut out the divisions to see how she could re-jig the landscape. By this means a disjointed, structural landscape emerged, with the sea lower in one section than in another. Such movable horizons and sectioned landscapes have now become a feature of her work.

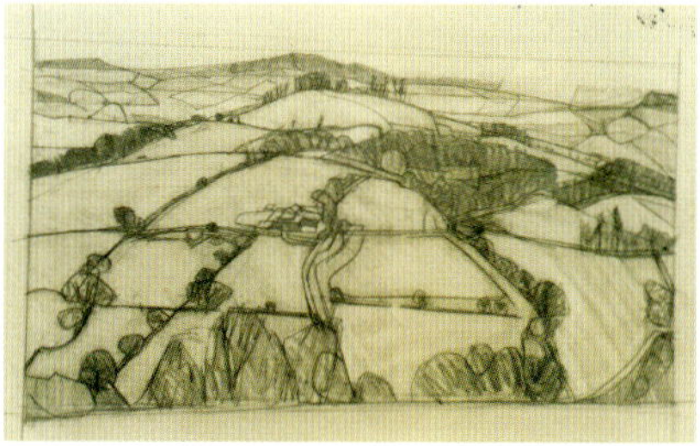

Drawing

Gardiner frequently refers to her drawings while painting in the studio. She may suddenly look up and see something relevant which she can use in a painting. Her *Conegar Hill* paintings of the early 1990s are relatively figurative. They are painted in acrylic but have additional collage material. She once wrote (Duncan Campbell Catalogue, 1992), that the introduction of collage into her paintings assisted in the refining process; it made the image less descriptive but more harmonious and precise in feeling. In many paintings of this period a range of greens predominate, with autumn and winter browns, fawn-pinks and reds of ploughed earth and tracks. Highlights of white also figure, they trace ribbon country roads and exposed chalk layers. However, after a while, greens in particular started to disappear from her palette, this was accompanied by an equivalent rise in the use of blue. At the same time, in paintings such as *West Dorset Landslip* (1992/93), she began to divide the landscape into detached, irregular sections; each one 'islanded' by white paint. This approach to breaking up the landscape has since been increasingly developed in her Boscastle paintings.

At the same time that Gardiner was experimenting with sectioning landscape she began to use a vertical format. She found it, as she still does, a demanding format. However, it contributed an increasingly abstract element to her work and she still continues to experiment with it, as in the more recent painting, *Vertical Coast 2* (2000). The Field

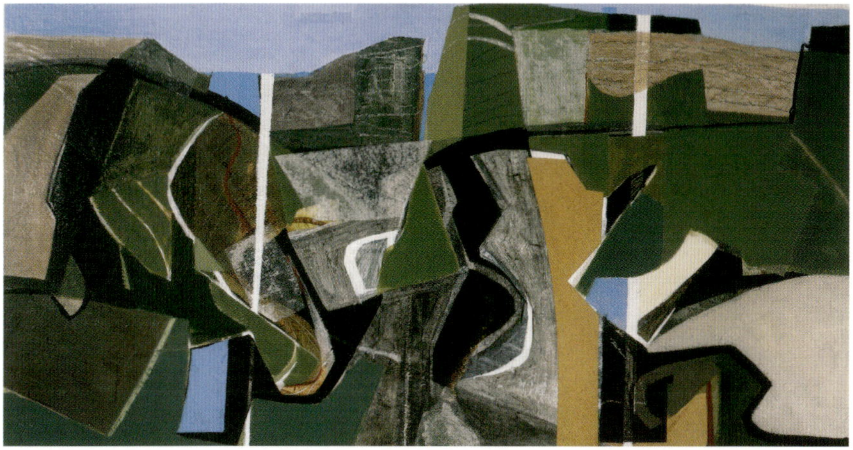

Eggardon Hill (1992)

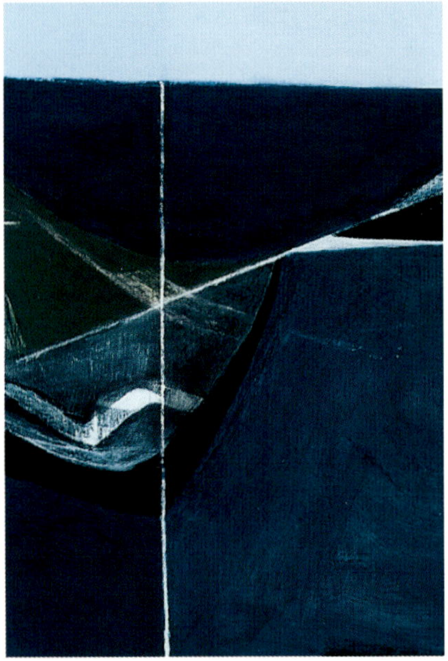

Detail *Harbour Coast, no. 7* (1997)

Paintings of Swyre (*Hanging Fields*, 1993) and Pucknowle are perhaps the closest that Gardiner has ever come to producing paintings which are purely abstract. Whilst continuing to work with inland places she came to realise that there was a connection to another location which she knew well. This location was Boscastle and Forrabury Common, with its Celtic stitch-field system.

Gardiner had continued to visit Boscastle since her early childhood family holidays. Now in the mid 1990s she began to paint and draw there more intensively. These paintings have a Cornish affinity with Michael Canney's coastal and harbour oils of the late Fifties and the Sixties. Gardiner has always admired Canney's ability to combine a softness of abstraction with an emotional connection to colour and place. For this reason she has also admired the work of Ben Nicholson, Keith Vaughan, Alexander MacKenzie, Adrian Heath and Peter Lanyon.

Working in Cornwall, Gardiner began to realise that for some time she had been trying to make the Dorset landscape a more dramatic place than it actually was. Black Ven had certainly provided drama, but Boscastle offered a tauter, more powerful landscape. Boscastle sits on a spectacular stretch of the Atlantic coast, which Hardy described as being the colour of opal and sapphire; a place where chasmal beauty looms in a wild weird western shore (Beeny Cliff)[9]. The geology is hard granite laced with seams of white quartz and specked with mica. It is uncompromising territory. The inlet is narrow and fjord-like, while above, the panorama is open, strange and wild. It is from the elevated heights above Boscastle, that Gardiner now mostly draws, and it is these drawings which presently feed her work.

Today, Gardiner's pictures are always constructed pieces as in *Harbour Coast, no. 7* (1997). She no longer works with oils, finding that acrylic at present suits her best. She paints directly onto marine plyboard which she first primes and makes some kind of drawing on. Certain areas of the board are then painted and left to dry. Once dry, surfaces are worked on with wire wool, sandpaper and other abrasive material. While 'sanding-back' she decides what other areas might need more paint, which areas are beginning to get the veiled effect she wants, and so on. It is an ongoing, concentrated process which takes many re-workings and re-paintings. Some surfaces are only lightly worked while others receive hours of attention. She usually works on four or five different pictures at any one time. Painting on plyboard, means that a colour, once applied, is difficult to completely eradicate. The plywood's grainy surface holds on to specks of paint even after severe rubbing back. This particular element is a quality that Gardiner exploits; it allows both intentional and accidental surfaces to emerge and for the piece to retain something of the history of its making.

Gardiner's colours are those of the land and the sea with a dominance of sea greens, blues and greys with touches of bronze and brown. "White is an aesthetic pleasure; it's something that's emerged in association with the idea of paths, of wearing down to something else. It also has to do with the sea as it hits and surrounds the rocks." Paths are very important in Gardiner's work. White and red lines denote where people walk, there is a real scoring of the earth. These colours are also an accent, a visual part of the painting.

Perhaps the most striking and distinctive hallmark of Gardiner's compositions is the cutting up of the original painted board into several, often four or five, sections. These sections become the equivalent of the many views one experiences when walking out in a landscape. As Gardiner argues: when you are following a path you don't just look at one view all the time, your gaze is constantly shifting. The cut sections are re-jigged time and time again until a juxtaposition of balance is achieved. Gardiner likes balancing structures: "that's partly why the cutting up process exists; to re-balance the picture and break it up so I can then identify accidents that appeal to me". Eventually, after further painting and re-working, the painting is completed.

Harbour Coast, no. 7 (1997)

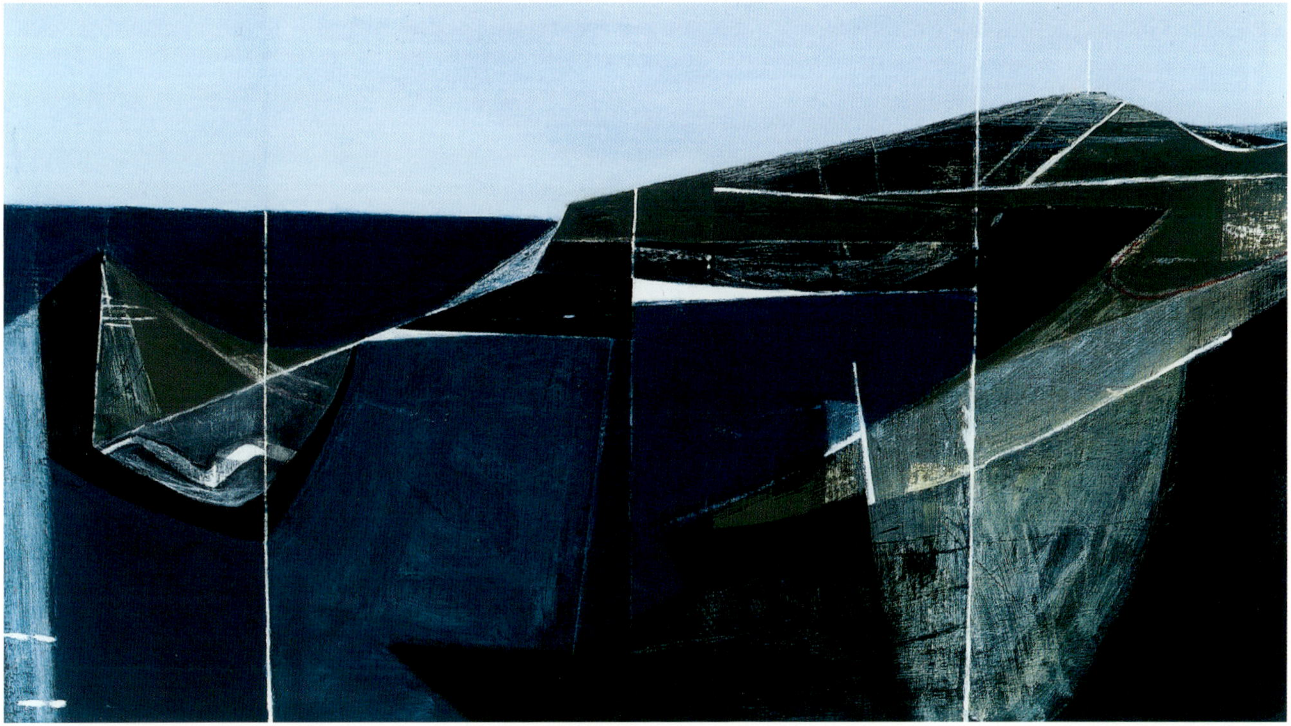

Cézanne is a painter that Gardiner has always admired for his intrinsic feel for the landscape. It is this feeling that Gardiner identifies with. She has only ever been interested in landscape. Very rarely has she ever painted people. "When I put a figure in the landscape the whole meaning of the place changes, the emotion of the place changes at once." It is important for her to have an intimate knowledge of any landscape she is working with; to be able to go back without any drawing and still know exactly where everything is. "It is important, because in a way that leaves you freer. By knowing one small area very well, you're freer to do more with it than if you know more, less well."

Gardiner believes much of her work to be as intuitive as consciously intellectual. Her task, as she sees it, is to translate the 'actual' landscape into a painting. To do this successfully, the landscape with which she works has to generate a great sense of excitement. As long as it does this, she will continue working with that place. Her paintings have an immediate appeal, and a connection to the natural landscape. Results are achieved by selecting out that which intrigues, and ordering it with sensitivity and emotion.

At some stage, Gardiner expects to return to what she describes as the "extraordinary, diverse landscape of Dorset", but for the moment Boscastle holds her attention. In some ways she believes it leaves her at liberty to enjoy living where she does in West Dorset. Here she can paint with few interruptions. Perhaps she is in the minority amongst contemporary painters in being happy to be known as a landscape painter. However, as she puts it: "the work is about the landscape and that's what I do. I'm just painting what gives me an enormous lot of pleasure. My paintings relate to that."

Biography

1960	Born Oxford
1978-79	Oxford Polytechnic: Foundation Course
1979-82	Central School of Art & Design: BA (Hons) Fine Art
1999-00	South West Arts: Fine Art Award
2000	Bournemouth University: Arts Loan Collection
2001	Bournemouth University: Arts Loan Collection
2001	Represented by Hart Gallery, London

Selected Solo Exhibitions

1991	Duncan Campbell, London
1992	Duncan Campbell, London
1993	Gordon Hepworth, Exeter
	Duncan Campbell, London
1996	Gordon Hepworth, Exeter
	The Town Mill Gallery, Lyme Regis, Dorset
	Duncan Campbell, London
2000	Duncan Campbell, London
2001	Hart Gallery, London

Selected Group Exhibitions

1991	Bridport Arts Centre, Bridport, Dorset
1996	'Art 96' Business Design Centre, London
1997	New Ashgate Gallery, Farnham
1997	Alpha House Gallery, Sherborne, Dorset
1999	Six Chapel Row Gallery, Bath
1999	Merriscourt Gallery, Oxfordshire
1999	'Art 99' Business Centre Design Centre, London
2000	Arts in Hospital, Dorset County, Dorchester
2000	Alpha House Gallery, Sherborne Gallery
2000	Hart Gallery, London
2002	Forthcoming: Alpha House, Sherborne, Dorset Arts Week

Public Collections

2000	Bournemouth University

Literature

Modern Painters magazine - review by Elizabeth James

2000	Bournemouth University Catalogue (illustrated)
2001	Bournemouth University Catalogue (illustrated)

BRIAN GRAHAM

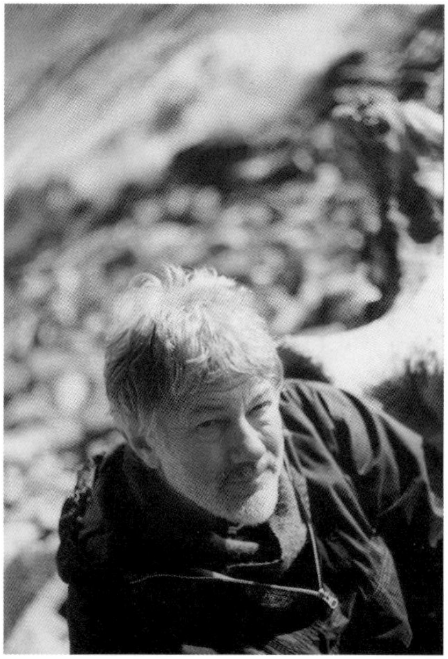

Just off the High Street in Swanage there is a lane almost too narrow for cars. This lane climbs steeply to join a road which leads westward to Durlston Head. This promontory is where a gigantic Portland stone globe of the world can be found; once used by Graham Sutherland on a Shell poster. At right angles to the Swanage lane is a tall brick house and it is here that Brian Graham and his wife Carol live. Graham's studio is on the third floor; it has white walls and a white floor. From the north-facing window there is a view towards the chalk stacks of Old Harry Rocks and the high ridge of Nine Barrow Down. Weather conditions are always changing in this landscape. On occasions, the whole escarpment is shrouded in a creeping, cloying mist. Another day will see dramatic explosions of light, and, now and again, storm and tempest will deny its very existence.

Graham lived in Bournemouth and Poole before moving to Swanage in 1993. Not far from his house is No.2 The Parade where the painter Paul Nash once lived. Nash had a mixed affection for the town. He found it a place of fascination, where grand imported London architectural artefacts jostled alongside humbler everyday buildings and the working equipment of fishermen, quarry and port workers. Nash's interest quickly manifested itself in a series of surrealist Dorset paintings during the mid-1930s.

Graham is "local born, if not of local stock". However, although born in Poole, Graham's parents came from London, only moving away from the city to escape the war-time bombing raids. Going further back in family history, his grandparents came from Cumbria and Cornwall. Graham went to Poole Grammar School and, showing early promise, it was suggested to him that he might become a commercial artist. He started as a junior artist at a design studio. "Instantly I came into contact with artists who had varied but considerable skills and I had to assimilate this professionalism very quickly. I was taught to think as well as do. How could creative ideas be best resolved within tight budgets and even tighter deadlines? Quite a grounding." After three years at the studio, Graham went on to a career in advertising which lasted until the late Eighties. He then decided, having several successful exhibitions behind him, to leave secure employment and paint full-time. His first exhibition, with Paul Jones, was in 1979 at Poole Arts Centre.

Not having received a traditional arts education, Graham sees himself as being mostly self-taught. In the early days he did have various teachers: "They seemed much influenced by Paul and John Nash, Edward Bawden and Eric Ravilious." Such names have become linked to the Neo-Romantic movement of the 1940s. These artists, when

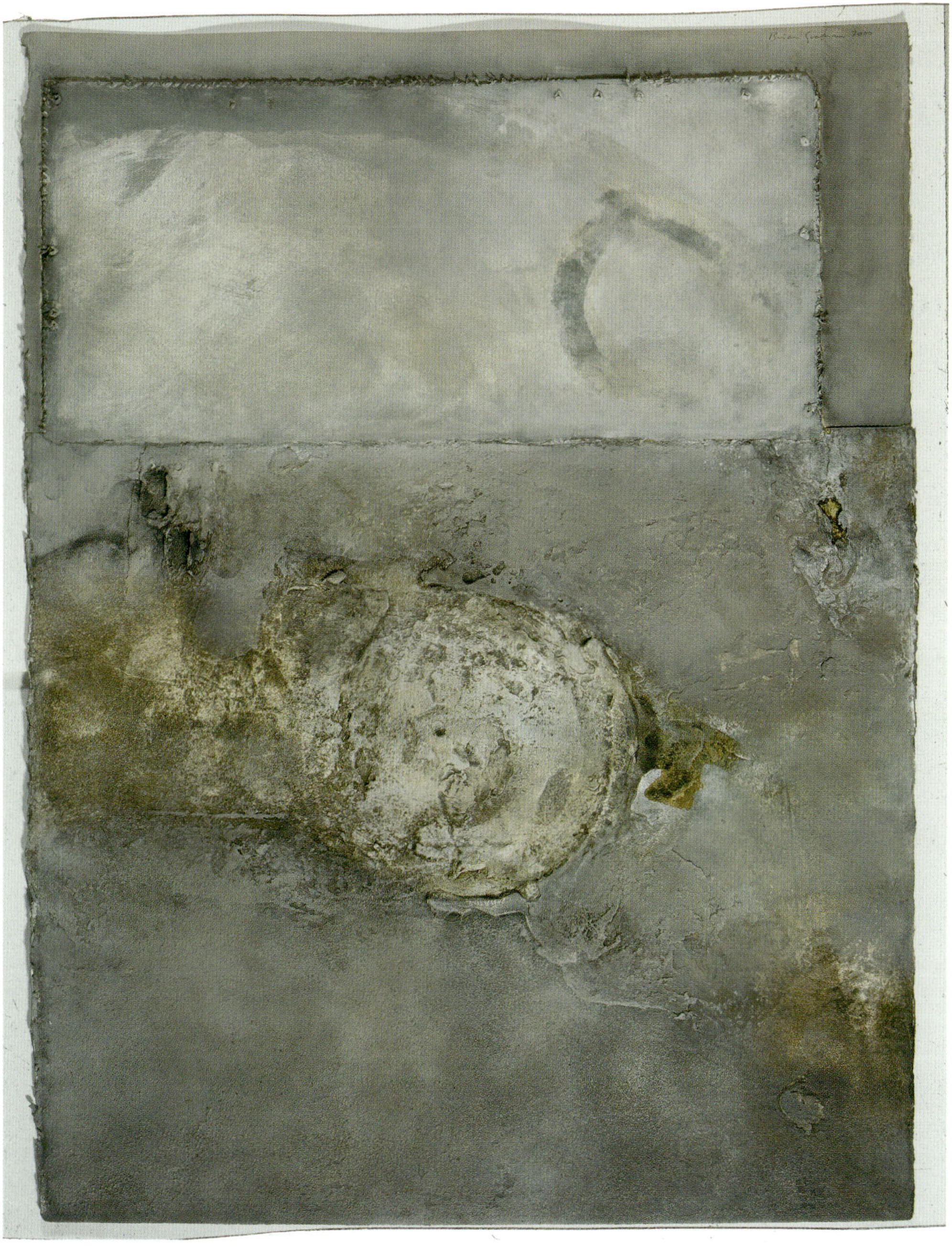

Ambulatory (2001)

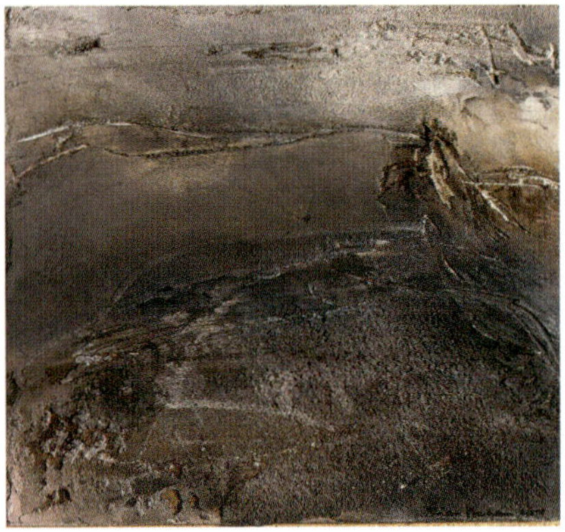

Landslip Hengistbury (2000)

not engaged as war artists, tended to retreat to small rural communities and immerse themselves in the local landscape. In selecting landscape as their subject they looked back to the latent English tradition of Romanticism. "The lecturers were kind and well meaning, but in 1961, aged just sixteen, I was confused by my joint exposure to a hard commercialism on one hand and the dying remnants of an art school system on the other."

Paul Nash, in particular, has been an important figure for Graham. Nash held that the motive power, the spirit of English art, was 'of the land'. He loved everything that was spiritual, magical and poetic; he explored beyond the obvious into worlds beyond. Although Graham has not followed in the surrealist steps of Nash there is an empathy with Nash's vision of the landscape. Both Nash (d.1946) and Graham share an affinity for remote locations; for places which were once occupied by people but now lie uninhabited and empty of all but the barest archaeological artefacts and traces. For Graham these sites, some showing signs of very early occupation, maintain a strong, palpable presence. They are places from which a highly charged but indefinable atmosphere emanates.

Graham's paintings are rarely representational, although they often draw on elements abstracted from life such as: graffiti scratched onto massive church pillars, roughly hewn marks on blocks of stone and curved outlines of hills. He finds his material all around him: "The found objects, the noble landscape, the tidal shoreline, the ancient and well-remembered hills." Some paintings do contain definable forms, some are even site-specific such as *Landslip Hengistbury* (2000), but more generally: "they're to do with inner potency and an overall sense of place".

The town and port of Swanage is a sheltered place. It is gathered round a bay which is protected from the prevailing wind. At the bay's north and south extremities, two massive ridges, one of chalk, the other of limestone, reach back inland like extended arms. It is this landscape and the coast which extends from Peveril Point, with its tide race, to Hengistbury Head, which helps to inspire Graham's work. Almost daily he walks part of the coast or the down. "Regular acquaintance allows greater understanding; the opportunity to observe the familiar in a new light. Sometimes places or configurations suddenly reveal themselves as significant. Without regular walking that probably wouldn't happen."

When he begins a painting, he often has no idea how the finished work will be resolved. He does not need much to start with; a small charcoal or conté drawing of a simple shape such as a hollow in the ground, or an ancient vessel or tool. Once started, he has something to respond to. Gradually, he builds texture and composition by adding and subtracting paint. Edges of forms recede into vanishing backgrounds, leaving just enough outline to give shape and life to the painting.

Graham's palette is generally that found within the strata of the Earth: "You see an abundance of yellow and red ochres, greys, russets and whites. Mauves, blues and greens do appear from time to time but they tend not to dominate." He admits to "a passion for red." Some of his paints may be at the very dark end of the palette but he uses them to bold, dramatic effect. Painters that Graham admires include Rembrandt, Rothko, Bacon, Sutherland, Turner and Tapies. For Graham: "they all display an innate mastery of their medium, a supreme understanding of pigment".

Portland Inner Secrets (2000)

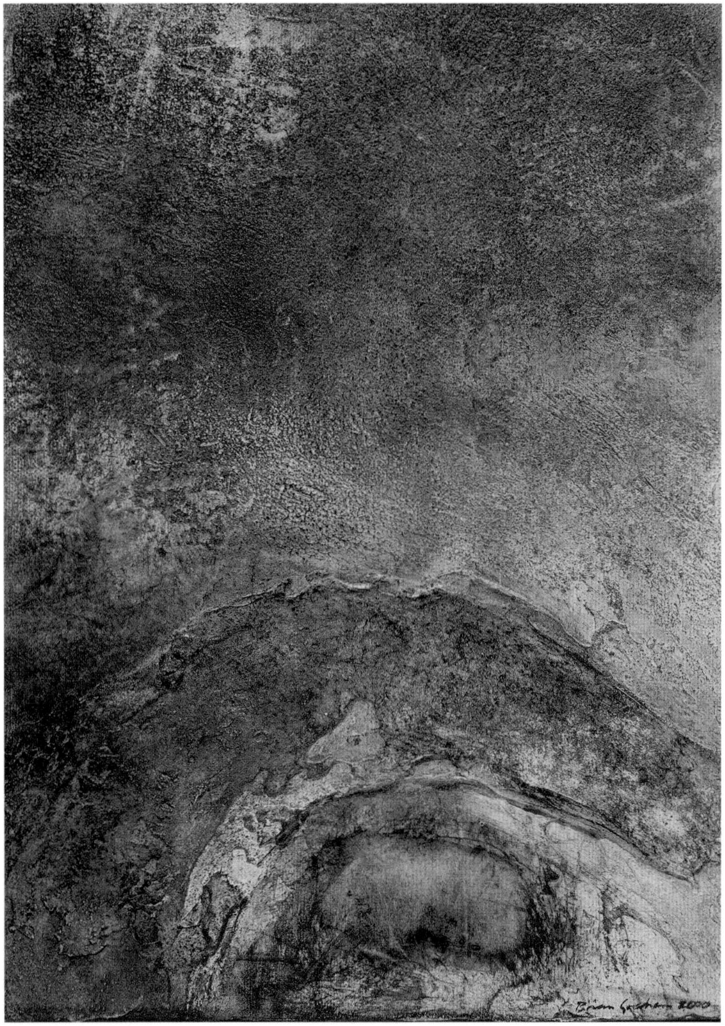

Graham's medium is mostly acrylic. This enables him to work with ideas quickly and to create exciting surface textures. "Paint is layered onto paint. Sometimes I use sand. I scrub, sand down, scratch across, draw and etch into, smooth down again and constantly repeat the process until I have something convincing. It can be aggressive; these delicate works of art are often the recipients of very rough treatment." Graham works with any one painting over a considerable length of time. To know when a painting is complete: "I have to trust my intuition and I do know. I recognise something significant has happened, but it is a dangerous time. The work has life, a presence, but needs completion. I cannot rationalise this moment of knowing but hope onlookers will join me in recognising something more substantial than the commonplace."

One constant source of inspiration for Graham has been the investigation of place. He is knowledgeable about the many Mesolithic and Palaeolithic sites to be found in Dorset and the borderlands of the county. A favoured site of his is the prehistoric harbour of Hengistbury Head, Christchurch. Another is Culverwell, near Portland Bill, where archaeologists have uncovered evidence of Middle Stone Age people. *Portland Inner Secrets* (2000) and *Portland Revealed Floor* (2000) are both Culverwell paintings. It is also from here that Graham's *Habitat* series of paintings originates. Moving further inland, Whitcombe Hill near Winfrith Newburgh and the remarkable discoveries made recently at Boxgrove, near Chichester, have provided fresh material for him.

Dolmens and stone rings have always held a particular interest for him. Sites he knows well are Kingston Russell Stone Circle, north of Abbotsbury; The Nine Stones, near Winterbourne Abbas; the Neolithic stone tomb of Hell Stone near Portesham; and the Megalithic burial-chamber of The Grey Mare and her Colts just south of Little Bredy. At such sites Graham makes many drawings, essentially for placement and positioning. They provide him with a starting point, an architecture upon which to hang ideas and to explore form.

These ancient sites have an acute potency for him. He finds them immensely powerful places. "The hinterland of Cranbourne Chase resonates with the distant past. The well-known, like Badbury Rings and Ackling Dyke make their own case, but just being in this unique landscape can be more than enough. Prehistory is all around, often beneath our very feet." There remains but fragmentary evidence of past habitation so it becomes a matter of detection, speculation and surmise. Today there is little left but a few artefacts, marks or traces. "Scraped recesses in the ground or the suggestion of post holes or darkened cave entrances leading into the limestone depths are the substance of what were once human dwelling places, sometimes temporary, often long-term. The paucity of evidence is so suggestive, so tantalising."

For this artist, the less there is, the more it offers his imagination. Graham's paintings, such as *Portland Revealed Floor, Glowing Hearth* and *Ashen Site*, are tangible constructs of unrecorded but archeologically evidenced human events and life. Through a process of re-invention Graham eventually finds a way into his subject. "Consider a Stone Age hunter-gatherer campsite. Centred on the hearth, the most basic of dwellings would be occupied by family and tribe. If I were to introduce these figures the illustrative content would be far too obvious and self-conscious, implying a knowledge of their ways, habits and appearance that we just don't have." Instead, it is through the physical act of painting, through the laying down of obscure mists of white or dark pigment shadows that a figure or entrance to a habitation may come into being. To these paintings there will always cling an air of suggested uncertainty, of un-closed resolution which perhaps mirrors the academic discipline of archaeology itself.

In Graham's paintings of the Dorset coast there is often a strong, warm, reflected light saturating the tops of the cliffs and chalk headlands. The source of the light is distant and speaks of the opening or closing of a day. The mood is quiet and the atmosphere calm. However, more recently, Graham has subverted such harmony with stormy skies and dark land. This change of mood has come with visits to the granite coast of Cornwall. In these more restless works, rising currents of air push hard across high ground, setting the sea and earth into agitated opposition. The use of selected translucent pigments deepen surface pockets of uneven ground and throw into relief opaque, dense areas of painted canvas.

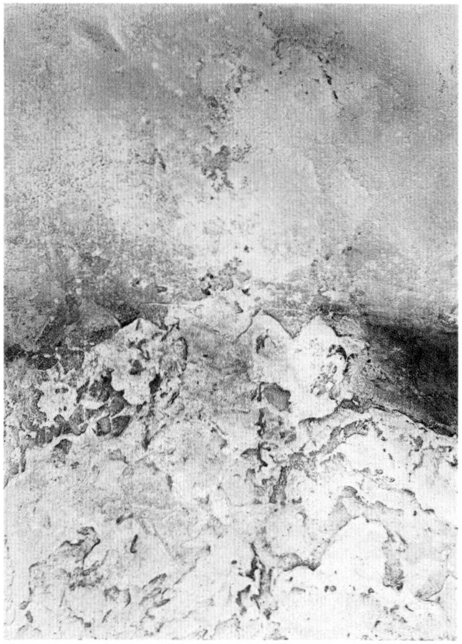

Portland Revealed Floor (2001)

Detail *Portland Revealed Floor* (2001)

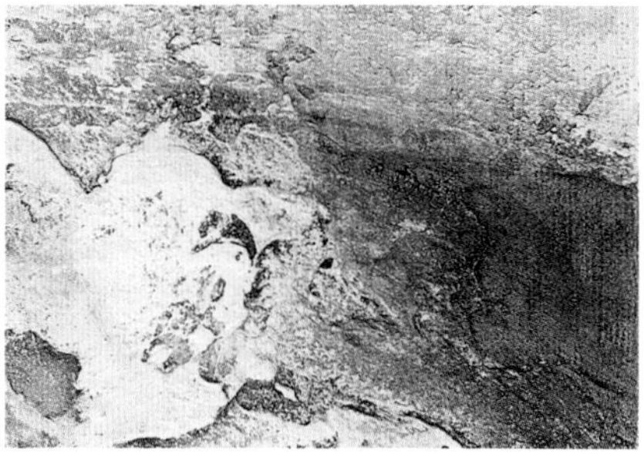

Graham is a keen beachcomber. Whenever walking on the shore, he cannot resist picking up interesting 'finds', which come in a variety of materials from metal and stone to bone, wood and wire. Some of these collected objects are hung on a wall of his house for a while: "They are such beautiful things, so self-contained, ready-made and absolute. They couldn't be better. Random perfection created by indifferent forces." He has used some of them directly, taking their shapes and textures for a series of paintings called *Musical Pieces*. He has also used forms observed in the exposed rocks along the shore-line. "Some years ago I started to consider how the forms of primitive musical instruments could be used as subjects. If fragments of potentially sound bearing artefacts were uncovered by a trained eye, one might speculate on their purpose - perhaps musical; but how would you play them?" Working through these ideas provided a change of scale from the *Habitat* series. It also prompted Graham to return to experimenting with creating a micro/macro world within a single painting. Combining these two extreme dimensions adds an edgy ambivalence of scale to any work.

Ultimately for Graham, however, everything relates back to the experiences generated by archaeology and place: "Although I have the privilege of living within this area so rich in prehistoric remains, I am concerned that my work isn't seen as parochial or purely topographical. The viewer will always bring their personal experience to a work, and previous collectors from Australia and the United States have recognised compelling parallels with their own often diverse landscapes in my paintings. The majority of my works are concerned with how the considerable passage of time has affected our landscape and how our distant forebears have teased us with the remaining fragments of their long-gone lives."

For Graham it is the one big subject: "Nothing else really excites me in the same way. It is, after all, full of possibilities. In the year 2000 I made a series of ten works on the pleasures afforded by the content and environment of medieval churches. In this case I was governed by a more recent timescale, but the motivation was just as strong. The subject compels me to work and my fascination with certain aspects of our past started when I was very young." This is what keeps him living in Dorset and gives emotional energy and joy to his work. "Here in my Studio I can see Nine Barrow Down on the north-west horizon of an immense grass and gorse coated chalk spine running out to the cliffs at Ballard Point. On a clear day the Needles on the Isle of Wight stare back across the water at me. This doubles as a magnificent distraction and an ongoing inspiration."

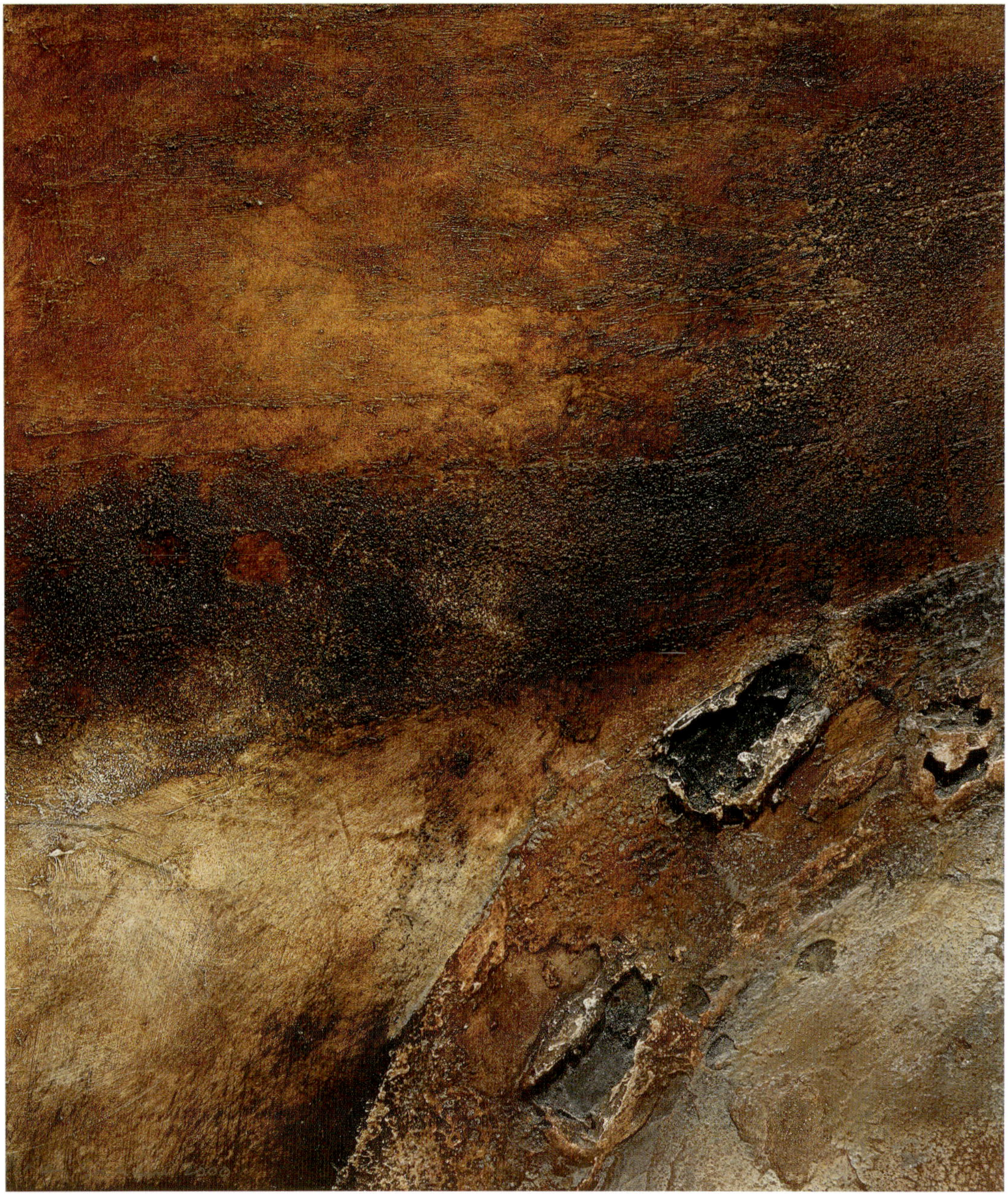

Patrolled Quadrant (2001)

Biography

1945	Born Poole, Dorset
	Poole Grammar School and (for brief period)
	Bournemouth and Poole Colleges of Art
1992	First prize, Royal West of England Academy
	Annual Exhibition, Bristol
1993	Moved to Swanage
1999-	Represented by Hart Gallery, London

Selected Solo Exhibitions

1986	Poole Arts Centre
1989	Dorset County Museum, Dorchester
1989-96	Alpha Gallery, Swanage (four exhibitions)
1992	Cleveland Bridge Gallery, Bath
1993/95	On Line Gallery, Southampton
1994	Atrium Gallery, Bournemouth University
1995-01	Bettles Gallery, Ringwood (five exhibitions)
1995	Gallery 27, Cork Street, London (presented by Contemporary Art Magazine)
1996	The Gallery, Cork Street, London (presented by Parnham House)
1999	Hart Gallery, London
1999	Hart Gallery, Nottingham
2000	Hart Gallery West, Cornwall
2001	Hart Gallery, London

Selected Two/Three/Four Person Exhibitions

1979	Poole Arts Centre
1990	Hann Gallery, Bath
1992	Christies Contemporary Art, Cambridge
1994	Cleveland Bridge Gallery, Bath
1997	'Art at 46' (presented by Lynne Green), Southampton
1997	Winchester Contemporary Art, Winchester
2001	Galerie Place Neuve, Vers Pont Du Gard, France

Selected Group Exhibitions

1990	*Paintings from Dorset,* Pelter Sands Gallery, Bristol
1991	Cleveland Bridge Gallery, Bath
1993	Art '93 - '99 , London (four exhibitions)
1993	*Painting the Earth,* The Gallery, John Jones, London
1994	Coram Gallery, London
1998	The Gallery, Cork Street, London (with Adam Gallery)
1998/99	20th Century British Art Fair (two exhibitions)
1999	Maltby Gallery, Winchester
2000	'Art 2000', London
2000	Bournemouth University Art Loan Collection
2001	20/21 British Art Fair, London
2001	Salon de Mars, Palexpo, Geneva, Switzerland
2001	Hart Gallery Artists, Leeds
2001	Galerie Place Neuve, Vers Pont Du Gard, France
2001	ARTeNIM Foire Internationale d'Art Contemporain, Nimes, France

Collections

Graham has paintings in both national and international collections - private, public and corporate

JOHN HUBBARD

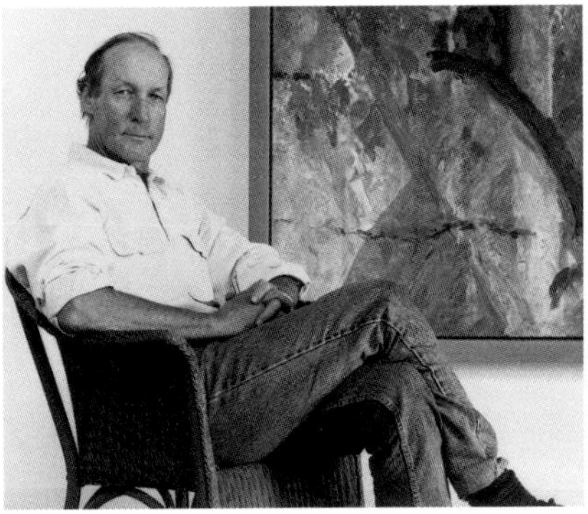

Chilcombe is a small hamlet tucked into a fold of one of West Dorset's round chalk hills. In 1980, Roland Gant described Chilcombe as comprising 'the eighteenth century farmhouse, the farm buildings, the studio of the painter who lives in the farmhouse, and two cottages along the lane'. Nothing much has changed since then and the painter referred to is still the same painter, John Hubbard, who came to live at Chilcombe in 1969.

Two miles due south of Chilcombe lies the sea and Cogden Mere, which is a lonely place on the Chesil. Up until the early Fifties few people visited; a cart and horse with a driver loading shingle at low tide might then have been the only sight. The Mere is an open, exposed piece of coast which is at the mercy of the elements. It is also a place that Hubbard has extensively used for his painting.

At Cogden Mere, the shingle of the Chesil runs in a straight uninterrupted bank (*Chesil,* 2000). In calm weather, the surf of the sea laps the shore sometimes leaving a gentle, white-lace surf. In rough weather this edge is broken and breakers crash onto the shore with an echoing boom. Pebbles are dragged back in a dangerous undertow. This movement creates such a cacophony that at times no voice can be heard over it. Chesil is a place of contrasts; it can shine like gold on a sharp, bright day but when the mist creeps in, it disappears under a diaphanous mauve veil. The coastal fog is blanket-like, thick and enveloping, dense and cold.

However, in general, the light along the Chesil can be of a quality which is difficult to surpass. Here at the Mere, there are no cliffs or high vegetation to hinder the light; there is only the sea, the sky, clouds and open land (*Clouds, no. 2,* 2000). In his painting, Hubbard captures this radiance, this luminosity. He always starts with very thinned out paint, very open, very free, almost like watercolour. Then, gradually, the image starts to work. Textures and layers are built up over a period of time, using a variety of tools, from brush and knife to rag and fingers.

Hubbard enjoys walking, and inland from the sea there are quiet, green places to walk, such as the Plush Valley and the 'man-worked landscapes' of West Dorset. Among the latter are the ancient hill forts of Eggardon, Shipton and Hambledon: "They are marvellous, absolutely stunning and I make many drawings of them." Hubbard uses drawing as a preliminary to almost any painting activity. "It's a form of study, working

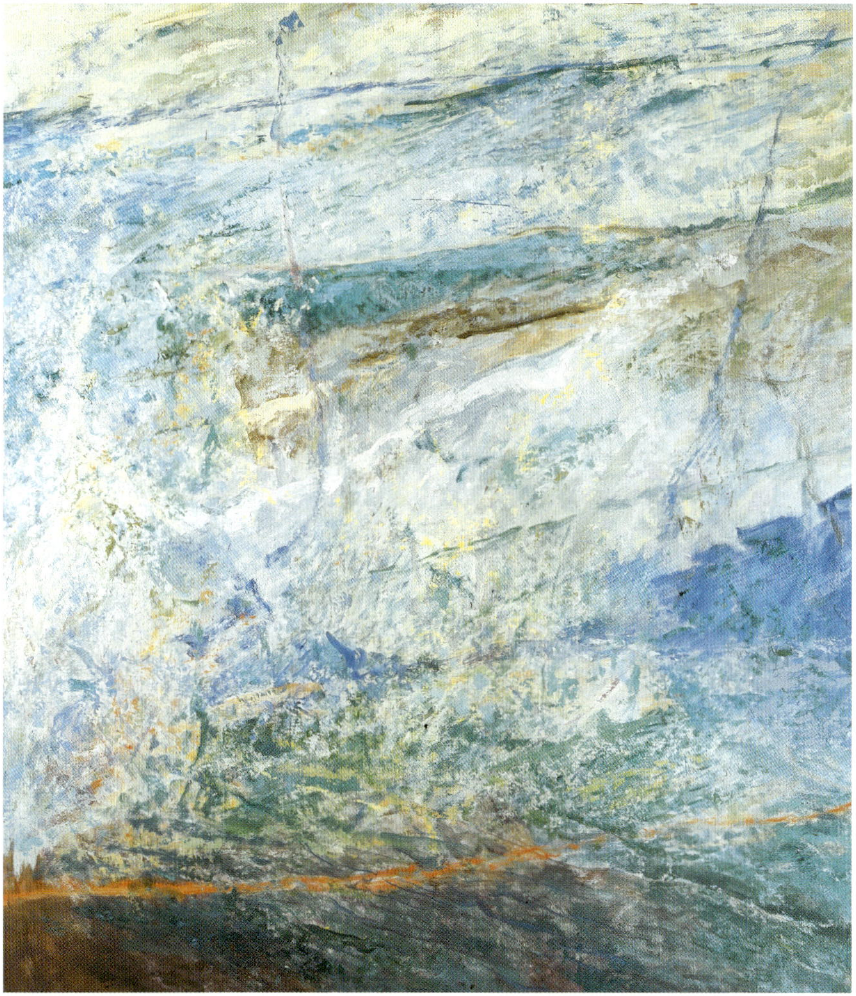

Chesil (2000)

one's way into it. The fact that one's working in charcoal is already in itself so removed, you're doing something which is completely unlike anything you are looking at. You're not trying to simulate anything. I really love drawing."

Dorset Landscape (1967), is an early Dorset painting, but the whole West Dorset landscape continues to arouse as strong feelings in Hubbard as it did when he first arrived." The landscape is like a wonderful, extraordinary piece of sculpture. It's got such a sense of movement and a kind of determination. It's this incredible mixture of natural and man-made." Even though chalk creates soft, smooth contours, it can still be quite awesome, and in spite of there now being more people, more houses, bigger villages, bigger towns, "you still get that sense of strangeness".

Hubbard has been involved with landscape for most of his painting life. Dorset has always been an essential background to his work, if not an ongoing subject. In the 1960s it was 'ninety percent Dorset' but in the early Seventies he wanted to broaden his understanding and use of colour. "I very much adhered to landscape colours when I was doing the Dorset paintings. I didn't put them together in a conventional way but they were essentially the colours of the observed world." It was a visit to the Atlas Mountains, Morocco, in 1969, that brought change: "the rich minerals ... the very extraordinary, mysterious colours and wonderful passages of light as the sun rises and sets and the mists fall; the rivers rushing through the passes, the mountains ...". Hubbard returned three more times to Morocco and for the first half of the Seventies, his paintings continued to be based on the Atlas Mountains.

After returning to Dorset, Hubbard became very interested 'in things to do with stones', including granite. He worked both on Dartmoor at Haytor and occasionally in Dorset. He also made charcoal drawings in his own garden at Chilcombe and in the nearby Sub-Tropical Garden of Abbotsbury. "Abbotsbury led me to Tresco in the Scilly Isles. Artist friends such as Patrick Heron and Tony O'Malley in St. Ives used to go there every year. I did a group of paintings based on the garden. Sometimes people find them rather too demanding and a bit assertive, almost aggressive. You get to the state when you feel that everything is growing at the expense of something else."

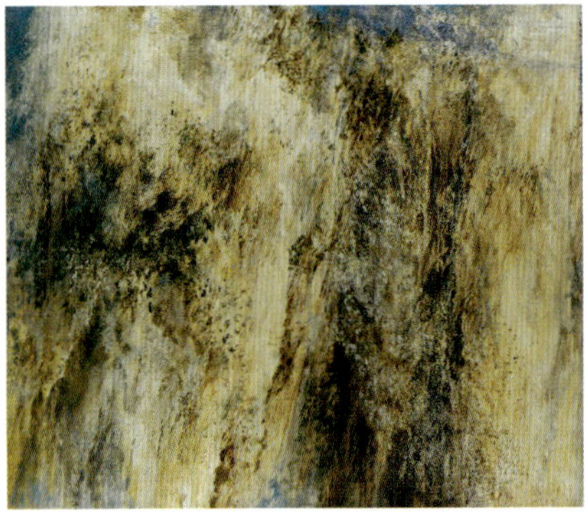

Dorset Landscape (1967)

Hubbard has always had a love of gardens. He was brought up in the countryside of Connecticut at Ridgefield, about sixty miles from New York City. "I was fairly solitary. We had neighbours but lived rather a quiet life. I spent a lot of time out in the garden, which was a wonderful, big garden, full of all sorts of things. That gave me a love of gardens; gardens as a kind of special place. The actual countryside was rather dull. Again, the garden itself, the immediate environment, was wonderful with wild flowers and so on and I was at my happiest in that context."

Throughout most of Hubbard's life there has been a strong sympathy with the Orient. This was first stimulated when he went to Harvard to read English, but also enrolled on a course in Art History. The latter fascinated him and he began to spend most of his time in the Fogg Museum (Harvard's Art Museum). "I became very involved with Ben Rowland, a Professor of Oriental Art, who also was interested in contemporary painting. He sent me to New York during my holiday to go round galleries and write reports of what I saw. So I went, and I remember the first show was Matta, a sort of proto-Surrealist, an architect by training ... Matta played quite an interesting part in the European/American art world at that time, although I wasn't to know that."

At the time he left Harvard the Korean War was ongoing. Hubbard enlisted in Army Counter-Intelligence and served from 1953 to 1956, spending most of his time in Japan. On leaving the army, he decided to go to the Art Students' League (ASL) in New York: "That's where it all started and I've never stopped. I studied mainly with Morris Kantor, who was a marvellous character, a great believer in what was happening, what was new. He himself had started as a sort of Faux-Primitive. He was very interested in Jewish subjects, being an emigrant Jew himself. By the time I crossed his path, he'd rather put that behind him and was very interested in all the exciting things that were going on in New York at that time."

"It was marvellously liberating. By that time, the New York School, the Abstract Expressionists, Pollock, de Kooning, Motherwell, Kline and all those people were in full flow. It was very exciting, there were a lot of galleries, a lot of debate. The ASL had teachers of every size, shape and description. George Grosz was teaching there. I studied with him very briefly, mainly drawing ... I found him very disillusioned with the world and embittered. He was also wonderful but a bit negative and I didn't want to study with the teachers who represented what seemed to me the old way of doing things. Then I studied one summer, 1957, with Hans Hofmann in his School at Provincetown, north of New York, out on Cape Cod. That gave me a kick in the pants, because Kantor was very kind and Hofmann was very brusque. The mixture of the two worked."

However, by 1958, Hubbard decided that the time had come to leave New York. He had been painting every day for two years but now he wanted a change, he wanted to visit Europe. First he came to England where he spent a month. During that time he went to St. Ives, prompted to go there by having seen the work of Peter Lanyon in New York. At St. Ives, Hubbard met many painters, including Karl Weschke, Terry Frost and Bryan Wynter. Before this visit to Cornwall he had never heard of Barbara Hepworth and had only been vaguely aware of Ben Nicholson.

Clouds, no. 2, (2000)

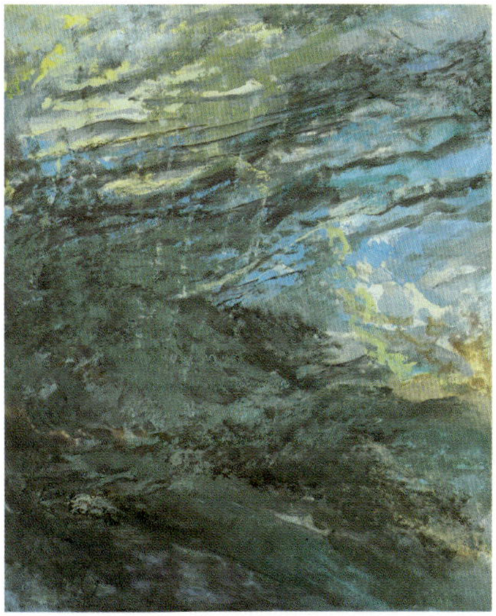

Leaving St. Ives, Hubbard then travelled to France, Spain and Italy. He finally established a base in Rome, where he stayed for two years. It was the offer of an exhibition in England, in 1961, and meeting his future wife Caryl, that led Hubbard to move to London, and then, after six months, to Dorset. "We came down here because we had an artist friend who said: 'You should go to Dorset, it's wonderful'. Reynolds Stone and his wife were friends of a great friend, and they said we know of a rectory for sale and there are other places. So we thought, 'let's go down and look'." Hubbard co-incidentally, as a child of the era of Life Magazine in the early 1950s, had read a photographic essay on Hardy country and been very taken with the black and white photographs of the Dorset landscape.

He remembers that finding their way to Dorset "must have been the most inspired bit of map reading. I don't think we had an ordnance survey map with us. On a fantastic day we drove down through Cranborne Chase and Milton Abbas and arrived at the coast by coming up a little track over Eggardon Hill. Don't ask me how we did that! In those days it was dirt, not made up at all. I remember we drove up and it started raining, there was a thunderstorm. When we just got to one of the little pull-ins at Eggardon, I said, 'Let's just stop', we were exhausted, overexcited; 'let's just have a little snooze'. So we shut our eyes, sitting in our little 2CV and were woken up by the sun shining in our faces ten minutes later. It was just a fantastic day. From then on, every minute got better and better. We came down over the hill and there was the sea, found our way to Litton Cheney and went and visited the Stones and we booked into the Ilchester Arms at Abbotsbury. They said there are two houses we know of and tomorrow we'll take you. Going towards Abbotsbury we went through Swyre, with a sign saying For Sale. I looked at it and said, that's it! Let's buy that house. We'll find out how much it is and whether we can afford it: £5,000 with half an acre of land. I was just enraptured by Dorset and I still am'. (The Hubbards later moved and bought Chilcombe, a mile or so away, in 1969).

It was now that Hubbard's Eastern and Western worlds of painting began to come together. On the one hand, there was Chinese landscape, with painters who painted landscapes in their studios but who lived in the country. "They had a contemplative attitude to life, to nature, to each other and to the world around them and the past and future." On the other hand, there was abstract expressionism which involved a 'plunge' into the subconscious to find imagery. To Hubbard there seemed to be a middle ground between the two. There was an overlap and he was interested to find how one could develop it. At the time he did not realise it would be through landscape; that realisation was not to come until a year or two later.

He recalls that: "In America, there wasn't much land-based abstraction as such. De Kooning started doing those paintings after I left New York but they were really not that much about landscape. They were much more to do with the making of pictures, about de Kooning himself, his personality, his way of working. They had high drama and they were very highly charged, powerful paintings. It seemed to me when I encountered artists here who were more landscape-based and who were also interested in what was happening in New York, that this was an area I could find my own personal way into. There were things to be done which I was quite surprised hadn't happened in America. It was one of the reasons I left. To be fair, there was early Diebenkorn, whom I didn't respond to, and Jon Schuyler, whose work I hadn't yet come across."

"When I actually started work in England, landscape-based abstraction was already considered to be passé by the Art Establishment, by art schools. This was the early. Sixties. It's strange and to some extent still true. However, it's perfectly understandable, because it was so dominant, with people like Paul Nash, Sutherland, Piper and so on, right up to the post-War era. I think a lot of people felt it had had its day. But to me, anyway, that wasn't part of my tradition. If I had been English born, I don't know that I'd be doing what I'm doing now. One can only guess, but I'm not sure. The fact that I could come to it from outside and didn't have this history helped."

"There were hardly any landscape painters to the fore by the time I studied in the late Fifties. The only one figure of some eminence was a very good artist called John Marin

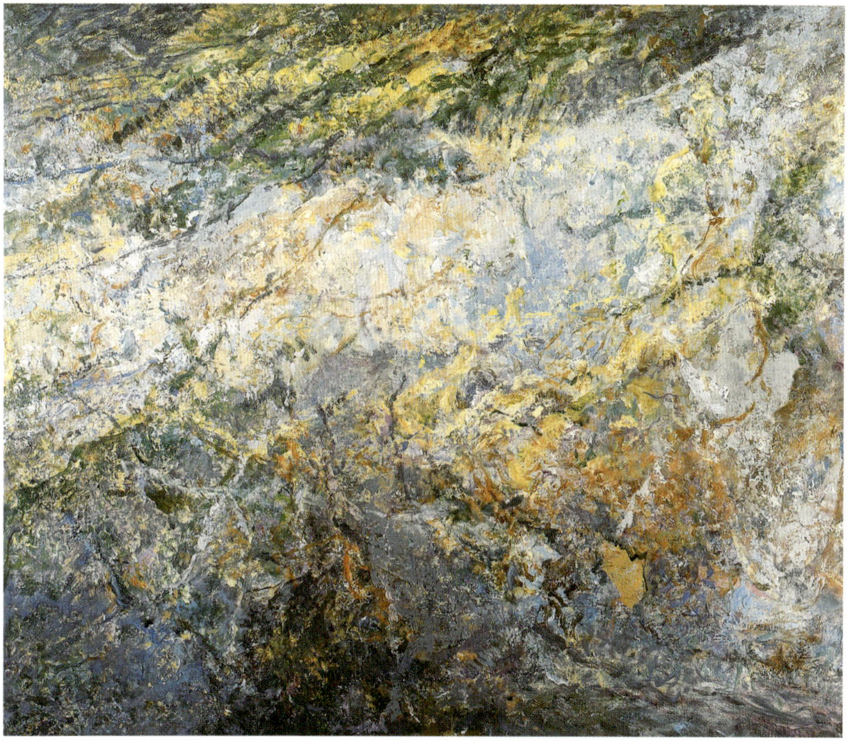

Cogden (1999)

(b.1870)." Marin worked most of his life in Maine, mostly painting in water colour. Similar to many of the great Chinese painters, Marin 'suggested' landscapes, using a kind of shorthand to reveal the essence of a place in abstract terms. He said that: 'the true artist must perforce go, from time to time, to the elemental big forms - Sky, Sea, Mountain, Plain - to re-true himself up, to recharge the battery. For these big forms have everything. But to express these, you have to love these, to be part of these in sympathy' (Munsterberg, 1951).[10]

In the first half of the Nineties, Hubbard spent a considerable time in Argyll, Scotland. He would stay for up to five week periods, always working in the same place. The result was *Scottish Paintings* 1993-96, which were exhibited in Ayr, Edinburgh and London. These estuarial paintings have to do with the extraordinary skies and seas of the place. Having worked on this theme, when approached by Dorchester Hospital for a commissioned work, he decided to pursue the same idea and Cogden Mere, so close by, seemed the obvious place. The *Cogden Mere* paintings, including *Cogden* (1999), "are all rather sunny, optimistic, lyrical paintings". They are, as with the Scottish paintings, to do with light on flat, marshland, on water and grass, or light over stone. They are simultaneous

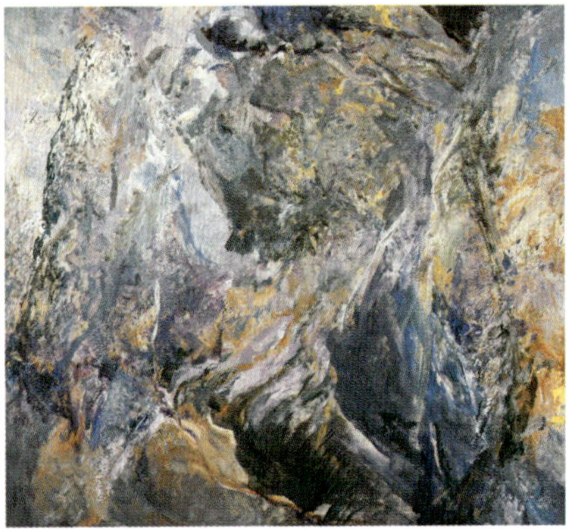

Lyme Bay (1996)

micro and cosmic worlds of organic and inorganic matter where scale is an unstable element. Hubbard says that people often comment that they seem to be based on small details, crusts of rocks or something like that or aerial views, but in actual fact, they are neither. "That they suggest such things is interesting. It isn't deliberate, it's partly how I see landscape. I constantly find it's shifting from what is close, what is immediate, to what is further off. I find that they exchange places all the time."

Hubbard's task has been not to concentrate on surface likeness, but to convey the abstract encounters of nature. Like Marin, his paintings 'breathe the very life of the scene potrayed' (Munsterberg, 1951).[11] In the Sixties, Hubbard's work was broader in concept. "Now they have much more odd detail in them and odd attention to bits and pieces, to corners and crannies. They are quite complicated spatially. A painting is unreal in a sense. One is creating not a perspectival space which was such a dominant thing for so long. Once you stop, cease to do that, you can create any space you want."

Today, Hubbard takes longer over a painting than he used to. When a painting is complete he will put it away for up to a month and then bring it out for re-assessment. Often he will do some fine-tuning, doing very small things which cumulatively make quite a difference. He recalls visiting Mark Rothko when he was working on the Four Seasons paintings which are now in the Tate. "Rothko showed me one and asked what did I think?. I said it was a very impressive picture, and he said, 'I think it's almost there but I've got to 'fatten' it up'. I didn't see that, it seemed to me to be fine but I was not the artist." However as Rothko talked, Hubbard saw exactly what he meant. "People talk about weight; a painting has to have a certain weight. Every painting has its own specific gravity. It's got to have that; without it, it isn't functioning as it should."

Hubbard feels that as he gets older he shies away from melodramatic landscape subjects. "To my mind this goes back to an oriental approach; things should reveal themselves over a period of time. I find that the time-scale needed for my paintings is very different from others. I was interested at one point in more dramatic paintings because that was part of Abstract Expressionism, tending to go for immediate effect, but that's something I moved away from a long time ago."

After forty years in Dorset, Hubbard's painting is still involved with the place. He likes the isolation. "Once I tried working in London but it wasn't good. In the studio I work with everything excluded. I don't look out of the window. I can't see out but I can look up through a large sky-roof window." Although he could happily work elsewhere for up to several months, essentially it is in Dorset that he paints and feels at home.

Biography

1931	Born in USA; educated at Harvard University
1956	Completed three years military sevice, based in Japan
1956-58	Studied at Art Students League, NYC and with Hans Hoffman
1958-60	Resident in Rome, travelled Europe
1961	Married and settled near Bridport, Dorset
1963-65	Visiting teacher at Camberwell School of Art
1968	Designed décor and costumes for Dutch National Ballet Production *Le Baiser de la Fee*
1969	First visit to Atlas Mountains
1970	Participated on various panels and boards such as the AIR, SPACE Southwest Arts and the Arts Council
1981	Subject of film for South Bank Show
1983	Designed décor and costumes for Midsummer, Royal Ballet, Covent Garden
1988	Resident artist at the Poet's House, New Harmony, Indiana
1990	Guest of the National Gallery of Malaysia
	Designed courtyard garden for West Dorset Hospital, Dorchester
1991	Water Garden (Coloured etching and carborundum) commission for 3i plc.
1992	First visit to Argyll
1993	Advisory Panel Member, Tate St. Ives
1995	Commission for Smith & Nephew plc, London
1996	Winner of Jerwood Prize
1997	Selected and installed Elizabeth Frink exhibition, Dorset County Museum
1998	Commission for West Dorset Hospital, Dorchester
2000	Millennium Carpet Bedding Commission for Waddesdon Manor

Selected Solo Exhibitions

1961-75	New Art Centre, London (nine exhibitions)
1964	University of Leicester
1965	University of Birmingham
1966	St Catherine's College, Oxford
1968	University of Keele
1972	The Leas Gallery, Folkeston
1975	Mappin Art Gallery & University Library, Sheffield
	Aberdeen Art Gallery
	Ikon Gallery, Birmingham
1976	Plymouth Arts Centre
1978	Newlyn Gallery, Cornwall
	Fischer Fine Art, London (four exhibitions)
1981	Warwick Arts Trust, London
1968/83	Dorset County Museum, Dorchester
1984	Salisbury Festival
1985	Museum of Modern Art, Oxford
1986	Yale Centre for British Art, Connecticut
	Madeleine Carter Gallery, Boston
1987	Bernard Jacobson Gallery, Armstrong Gallery, New York
1988	Poole Arts Centre, Dorset
1989	Portrait of New Harmony, USA tour
1990	Curwen Gallery, London
1994	Purdy Hicks Gallery, London
1995	Charleston Farmhouse, Sussex
1998	*Eight Variations on a Drawing by Rubens* Fitzwilliam Museum, Cambridge
	The Luminous Coasts of the Sea Bridport Arts Centre
2000	Marlborough Fine Art, London Paintings 1996-2000
2000	*Art in the Garden,* The Rothschild Collection, Waddesdon Manor

Numerous selected group exhibitions since 1979
Most recent:

1999	*The English Landscape* Flowers East, London
2000	London Print Fair, Royal Academy

Collections Include

Arthur Anderson & Co.
City Art Gallery, Portsmouth
Department of the Environment
Deutsche Bank
Victoria and Albert Museum
Tate Gallery, London
Scottish National Gallery of Modern Art, Edinburgh
The Nuffield Foundation
New College, Oxford
National Westminster Bank plc.
National Gallery of Victoria, Melbourne
Art Gallery of Ontario, Canada
ICI plc.
Pearl Assurance
Ballarat Art Gallery, New South Wales
Fitzwilliam Museum, Cambridge
The Economist Group
The Financial Times
Devon County Education Committee
City Art Gallery, Bristol
Arts Council of Great Britain
Arts Council of Northern Ireland
Contemporary Art Society
Yale Centre for British Art, Connecticut
Thames Television
Smith & Nephew

PETER JOYCE

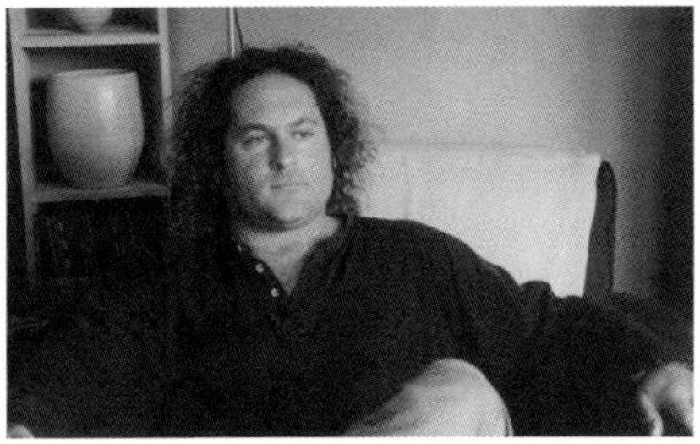

Peter Joyce owns stout walking boots. These are an essential part of his painting life. He is a keen walker and it is through walking he has come to know his subject well, his subject being the Isle of Purbeck, its properties, people and history. Although not a true island, Purbeck still has the feel of being bounded by water; of being a place unto itself. To the North lies heathland, to the West, marshland, whilst to the South and East are the waters of the English Channel.

Purbeck is a place of contrast and conflict. It can be windswept, bare and cold or lazily warm and lush. However, its limestone geology lends it a continual hard edge and whiteness: dry-stone walls, fossilised ammonites, sculpted cliffs, rough farm buildings, worn sheep tracks, tractor-harrowed trails and marble and stone quarries which lie near the sea's throat. Contrasting with this whiteness is the black of the rich oil: Kimmeridge oil shale, which first brought oil exploration and exploitation to Purbeck.

Joyce has a strong sense of identification with Purbeck. He was born not far away at Poole, an old town and port which today rubs shoulders with Bournemouth. Amoeba-like, Poole has expanded; there are new commercial ventures, industries and suburbs as well as an active ferry port. Poole's busy pre-occupation and pace of life stands in stark contrast to the emptiness of Purbeck, where the quiet is only disturbed by visitors in the summer months. Joyce has always had a deep love for the Purbeck coast and now, once again, he lives close by in Poole. Indeed, he lives in the very same house which was owned by his paternal grandfather: "It has come back into the family and all is much the same except, according to my father, the TV is in the wrong corner!"

Although the house may look the same, the contents are very different. Each room now overflows with ceramic pots, paintings and small sculptures. Many of the paintings are those of other Dorset artists. The collection of ceramics is large and pots spill out into the main hall, covering both shelves and floor. They are crafted by some of the best potters today, many of whom live in Cornwall. Joyce has a strong respect for makers who are good at the crafting of their art. When he buys a pot he enquires into the history of the potter: "where he's been, why he's been there, who he's been influenced by" and so on. This need to know the full story mirrors Joyce's own approach to his work.

Joyce knows a great deal about the Isle of Purbeck. This knowledge has been acquired over a lifetime and comes not only through reading but also through weekly physical exploration of the coast and its hinterland. Looking at the landscape, spending time with it is an absolute necessity for him. The landscape is not only a visual place but a sensory environment as well; a place where sound, touch and smell are as important as sight. Joyce's immersion of self in the landscape is reminiscent of Peter Lanyon (1918-1964). Lanyon spent most of his life in Cornwall and developed, like Joyce, an intimate knowledge of a particular landscape. Lanyon became a keen glider and in his layered and transparent abstract paintings re-created the sensations of flight: of wind and rain, of spiral air currents, tilted land and the unlimited boundaries of sea and sky.

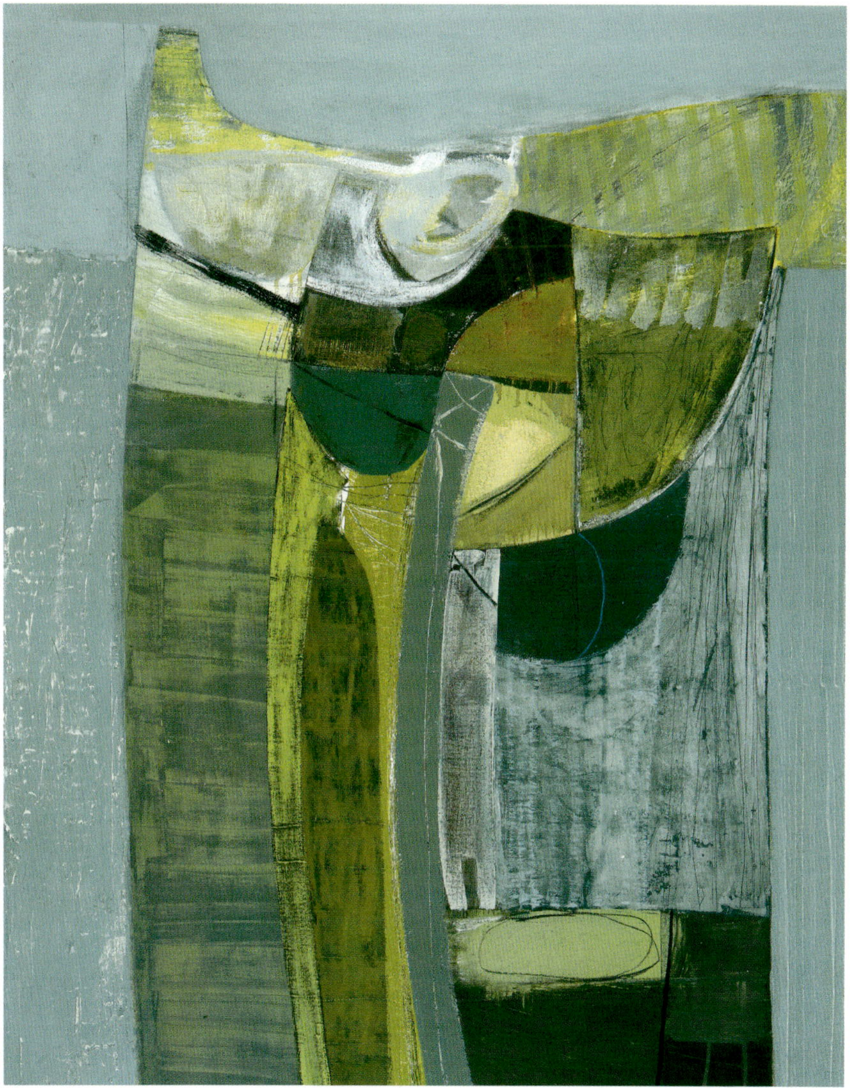

Windswept Walk (2000)

Joyce, although sharing something of Lanyon's way of working, has chosen a more topographic route when converting the physical into paint on canvas. Though both use an inherently aerial perspective, Joyce's paintings focus more on the physical land itself, its detail and its earth-bound qualities. Many of Joyce's paintings are named after actual walks, as for example *Windswept Walk* (2000). There is not the total synthesising of landscape which occurs in Lanyon; instead Joyce chooses to hold on to, for example, a particular landscape feature, a specific season of the year or an exact time of day, as in *Windspit Gloom* (2000). This is a man who cancelled arrangements for a weekend in order to stay out on the cliffs of Purbeck to watch storms come in from the tail-end of a hurricane. Joyce's paintings are indeed a kind of visual diary, and most receive a title containing a reference to a location.

From the age of six Joyce knew he was going to be a painter, although he was not quite sure 'what it was'. He never wavered in the idea that painting was to be his future and at

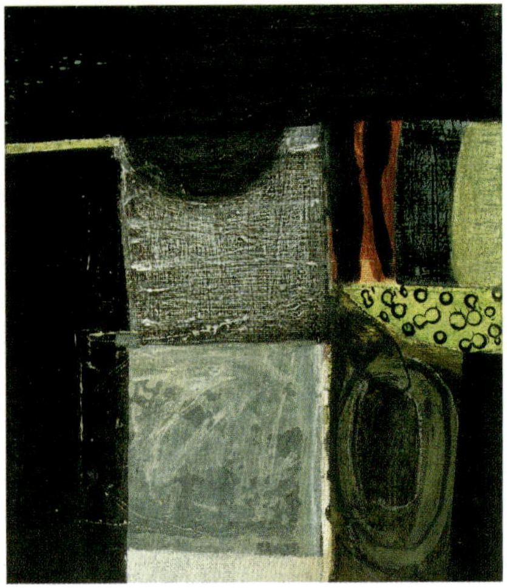

Windswept Gloom (2000)

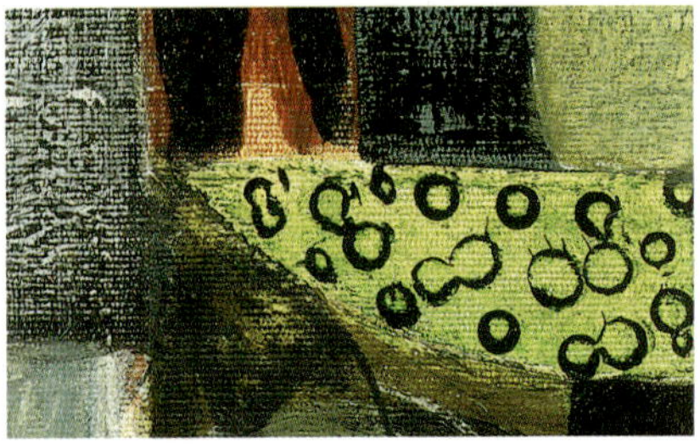

Detail *Windswept Gloom* (2000)

eighteen, he became a student on the Foundation Course at what is now The Arts Institute, Bournemouth. He then studied Fine Art at Stourbridge College of Technology and Art (1982-85) and subsequently was offered a place on the Masters Course at Goldsmiths. At the last moment, he decided not to accept the place. He reflects that if he had, it might have changed his work for ever. Goldsmiths at this time was turning its back on "good standard painting" in favour of "conceptual art, as practiced by Craig Martin and a young student there called Damien Hirst" .

However, having made his choice, Joyce struck out with determination and energy to paint alone, where and when he could. He moved back to Dorset and for the next few years divided his time between painting and temporary employment. He worked six weeks at a time as a labourer on a building site, earned as much as he could and then went off to paint, until the money ran out again. This pattern of life continued with frequent visits to exhibitions at London galleries until he had his first show with Anthony Hepworth in 1991. At the close of this exhibition he had only four paintings left out of fifty-two. From that time on he has painted full-time.

Joyce's paintings for the most part are abstract. Over many years he has invented a symbolic language which stands for land forms and shapes. These, he says, have been built on rules he has discovered for himself. Some forms translate easily, while others remain more elusive. Although there is no intention on his part for there to be a direct translation between what is seen in the landscape and what appears on canvas, some general connections may be observed.

Many a Joyce painting, such as *Purbeck Peninsula* (2001), begins with a drawn, block, isle-shape with water, or sky, on one or more sides. Bold linear lines, sometimes curved, seem to symbolize coast and land boundaries, while less weighty graphite marks become paths and track ways . Horizontal striations, in either paint or charcoal, denote strip-lynchets, ploughed furrows or rows of crops. Figures of eight, which complete on themselves, are plough marks in the fields. Other more solid shapes, such as the oval, circle or rectangle, originate from land sources such as small walled fields, round sheep pens, shell-marks in stone or pre-historic artefacts. It is from both the natural and tilled land, from farms and quarries, that Joyce draws his material. Their lines and shapes provide him with a beginning.

Initially Joyce begins a work by making marks on the canvas or board. "To begin with, I haven't got a specific location, I've got nothing else in mind but making a painting. I'm looking for a form, a drawing to start off with." It is through the process of drawing that access is gained to the 'bare bones' of the painting. "The formalities of paint and painting take over, along with considerations of the material, properties of paint, texture, colour and so on." Gradually the work takes on a life of its own and what next occurs

Purbeck Peninsula (2001)

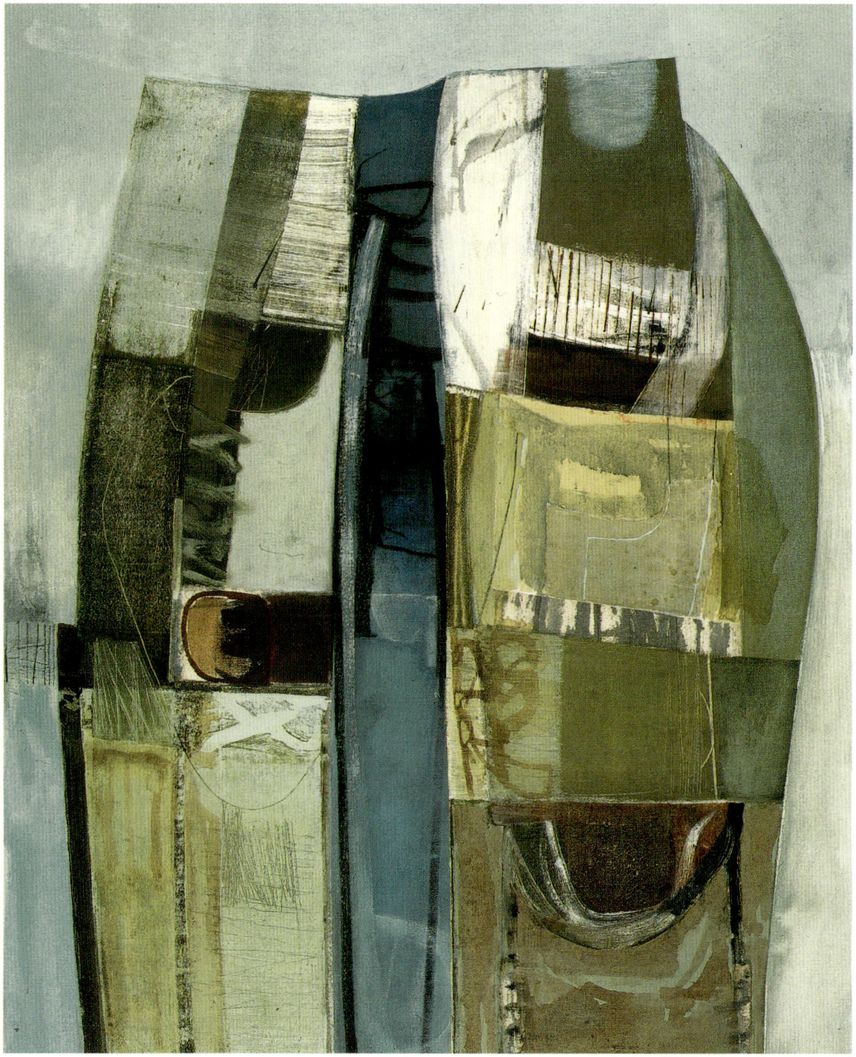

Joyce describes as a déjà vu experience. He begins to see connections to a particular place, to something familiar, to something once experienced. Once this happens, he can move forward, develop, and build the painting into a final composition.

The greatest joy of the Purbecks for Joyce has always been the limestone cliffs and quarries which extend all along the coast. The caverns of Winspit and Seacombe are favoured locations and "are equally fantastic from land or sea". From the sea, they appear as regular-sided black eye-patches in the cliff face. The nearby Tilley Whim Caves feature in the opening pages of Falkner's *Moonfleet* ... "The seams of Spangle and Grub ... you can walk in and see all those scenes you've read about, it's all there for you". Below these face quarries there are the broad dancing ledges where stone was once loaded on to flat bottomed-crafts and rowed out to ketch-rigged sailing barges.

By being familiar with Purbeck, Joyce understands "a bit more about the people, how they made use of the land, not just from the farming but the digging out of the stone". He surmises that if he had been born a hundred and fifty years ago, he would probably have lived at Kingston and been a quarryman, digging out the stone and dressing it. On past walks, he used to stop and talk with one quarryman called Mel Hayward. He had his own quarry which had been his father's and his grandfather's before him. Talking about the 'new' breed of quarrymen, Hayward once observed to

Joyce that whereas they would hit the stone twenty times to make it break, he just had to look at it twenty times and then hit it once. Joyce has found Hayward and his like a great inspiration. In many ways the quarryman's story epitomises Joyce's own approach to painting. Looking, really looking before putting something down on paper or canvas is at the heart of his work.

For over six years Joyce spent three days a week out in the landscape. Now this time is reduced. However, he still walks as much as he can and always carries a shoulder canvas-bag with him. When I inspected it, this bag contained, one paint brush; some tubes of olive green and white acrylic; tissue paper; oil and water pastels; fixative, glue and charcoal. In the past Joyce tended to do few drawings while out in the landscape, except drawings to record specific details. So, for example, an entry might be a drawing of "a flower, with five petals, with arrows pointing to details about how big it is, where the leaves come off and so on, or it might be of a bird seen from underneath, with interesting markings. Thus there may be lots of drawings, but not drawings of the landscape."

Recently however, there has been a sea-change. Joyce has begun to take time to do complete drawings and paintings at locations, such as *Above Topmast Quarry* or *Turf Rick Rock*. They are direct responses, and more figurative than abstract. For Joyce, who until now has always been a studio painter, this has been a completely different way of working. Searching for a reason for this change, he surmises it is connected to the way he works when in Cornwall or in Brittany. Here, when he draws, he has to grapple with a different landscape, one of hard unfamiliar granite. He has responded to the challenge by recording it figuratively, while at the same time searching for a new visual language to deal with the shapes and forms that are not in his existing dictionary of marks.

This figurative approach has now encroached upon his Purbeck painting. He is tackling new places, some of which he has previously avoided as being 'the too-obvious tourist places'. One location he has painted is a view from Studland towards Helstone Point, a view which takes in the chalk stacks of Old Harry Rocks. Such mixed-media works tend to be small. Many have a disjointedness about them since the sea, when viewed through the chalk stacks, seems to lack a constant level.

Besides these more occasional location paintings, Joyce continues to do his main work in the studio. Here, closed off from the physical world, he can focus solely on the activity of painting itself. "I tend to block out natural light and work in a constant light which is relatively low for an artist's studio." Controlling the light source not only frees him from changes in light quality but also differences in temporal light. "I can be working in my studio at eight o'clock in the morning and I'm potentially still there at ten o'clock at night."

His larger paintings are on 1.80m canvasses but generally he works on a smaller scale. In the studio he refers to neither sketches, or photographs; instead he allows experience and memory to surface. If he begins to struggle with a painting, he will make "a drawing to take out the colour, take out the tone and just leave the composition. Often the drawings stay, they're exhibited. Even though they are working drawings the painting doesn't come from the drawing."

Until 1993, Joyce used to paint with both oil and acrylic but having had to move house several times, he found oil-painting studios were just not portable, and so he became used to using acrylic in the way that he had previously used oil. Paint is neither thickly applied nor added to. Instead Joyce overpaints in continuous layers. Textures and marks, as in *Fishing Harbour* (1998) are crafted by whatever tool it takes to achieve the required effect. Scraping, rolling, brushing, knifed direct, all and any method of application may be used. Occasionally, he will also add collage material to a work.

His colours are mostly those of the sea and earth: blues, whites, greens, browns, ochres and siennas, colours that directly link to the landscape. Mauves and yellows, the colours of flowers and crops will also sometimes appear. Joyce is conscious that his colours exist within a fairly restrictive tonal range tending towards the subtle and quiet. However, as a result of spending time in Cornwall, richer hues and deeper colours are coming into his work, as in *West from*

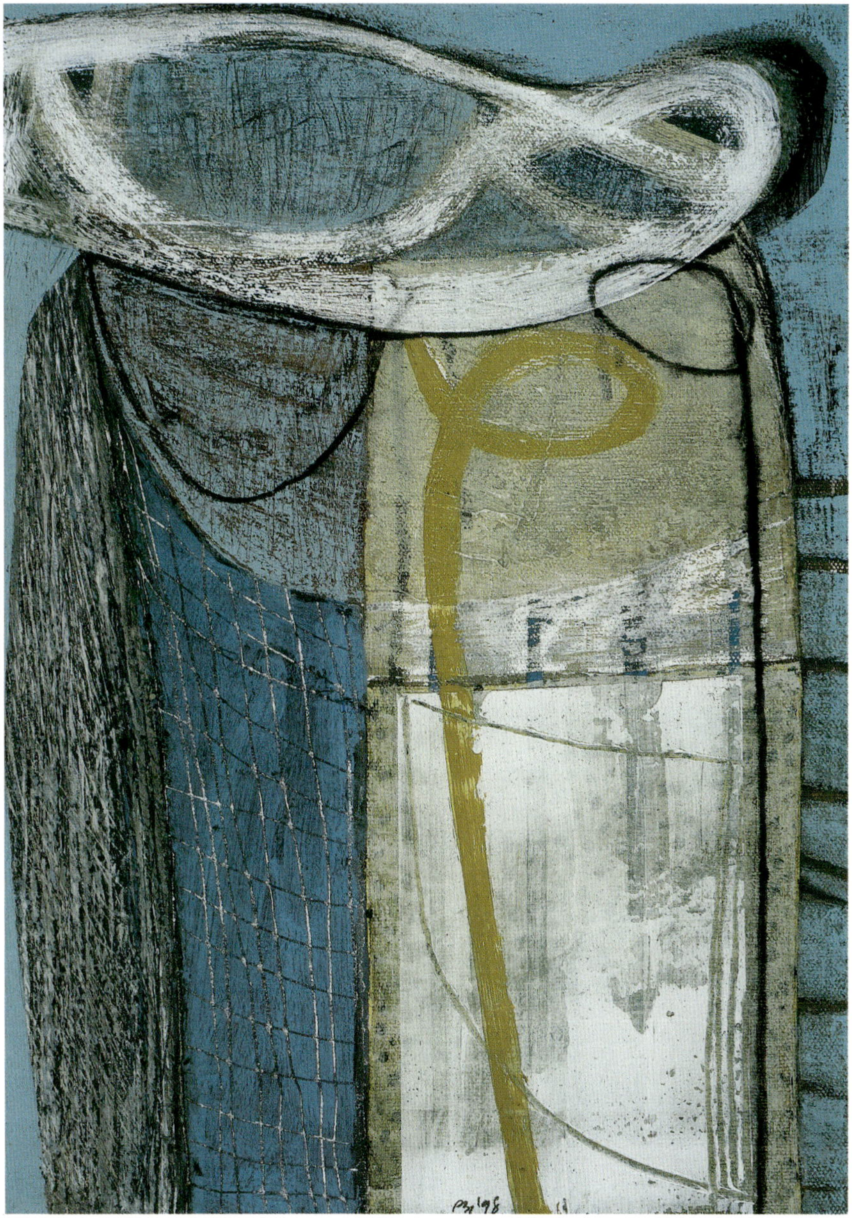

Fishing Harbour (1998)

Bodmin (2001). "I'm using colour for colour's sake as much as for the landscape. The considerations have become more abstract, in terms of colour, form and texture." There is also a less opaque quality to some of his Cornish paintings. Commenting on the sea near St. Ives he said: "It is as if they've left an electric light on and it's shining through". This more transparent quality is beginning to show in his Dorset paintings. There are certainly places along the Dorset coast where chalk beds slip out under the sea and turn it that same turquoise found along the north Cornish coast.

Joyce has now been painting in Dorset for fifteen years but he still does not tire of the place as a painting subject. Although new work is coming out from his visits to Cornwall they have made him appreciate the special qualities of Dorset. "They say Cornwall is a fantastic county, a wonderful quality of light and I'm not going to say, 'hang on a minute so has the Isle of Purbeck', because I really don't want them to know. Standing anywhere on that coast of Purbeck you are more or less surrounded by sea on three sides and there is an extraordinary quality of light, as there is in Cornwall. But there is also a greater variety of rock formation, of geology. As a natural habitat it's quite extraordinary."

West from Bodmin (2001)

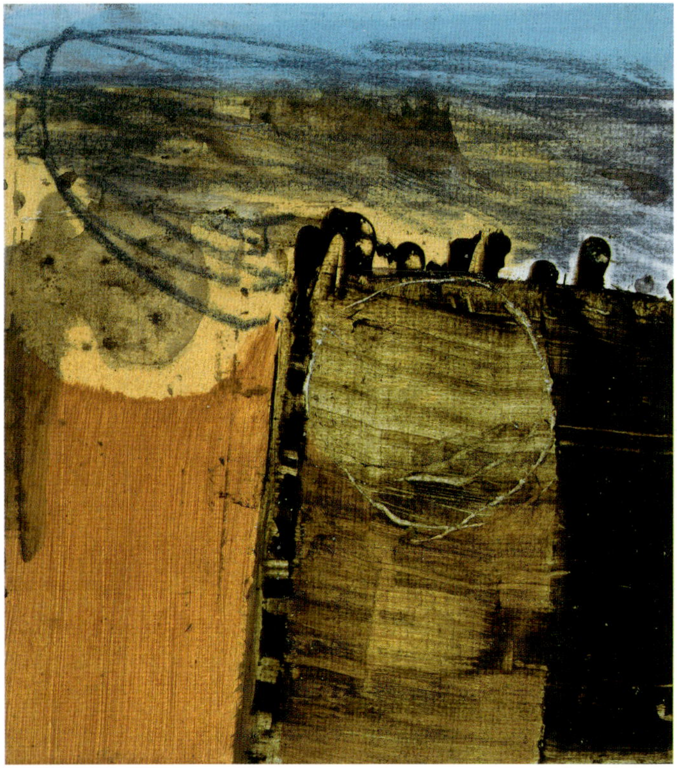

As far as Joyce can foresee, Dorset will continue to be his home and painting base. In an assured, direct manner he simply states: "My practice is painting and my subject the Dorset landscape."

Biography

1964	Born Poole, Dorset
1980-82	Bournemouth & Poole College of Art & Design
1982-85	Stourbridge College of Technology & Art BA (Hons)
1997-98	Chair of 'Room 10' Painters
1998 -	President of Bournemouth Arts Club
1998-01	Representative on Bournemouth University Arts Loan Working Party
1990 -	Represented by Anthony Hepworth Fine Art
1995-	Lecturer (30 days annual) Arts Institute, Bournemouth

Solo Exhibitions (since 1995)

1995	Ainscough Gallery, Liverpool
1996	'Head to Head', Russell Cotes Museum & Art Gallery, Bournemouth
1996	'Art & Archaeology' Cleveland Gallery, Middlesborough
1996	Anthony Hepworth Fine Art, Bath
1996	Bettles Gallery (with potter, John Leach)
1997	Alpha Gallery, Swanage
1997	Atrium Gallery, Bournemouth University
1998	Arts Institute, Bournemouth
1999	Bettles Gallery (with potter, Phil Rogers)
1999	White Gallery, Brighton (with sculptor, Anthony Hedgecock)
2000	Maltby Contemporary Art, Winchester
2001	Atrium Gallery, Bournemouth University
	Bettles Gallery (with potter, Mike Dodd)

Selected Group Shows

1992	CCA Galleries, Cambridge
	Art '92 - Art 2000 Contemporary Art Fair, London
1994	On Line Gallery, Southampton
1994/95	Laing Art Exhibition, Mall Galleries, London
1995-99	20th Century Art Fair Royal College of Art, London
	Olympia Fine Art & Antiques Fair
	Courcoux and Courcoux, Stockbridge
	Belgrave Gallery, St. Ives
1998/99	Juliet Gould Gallery, Cornwall
	Anthony Hepworth Fine Art, Bath
	Sanderson, George and Peach, Holmfirth
2000	EuroArt, Highcliffe Castle, Christchurch
	Four Seasons, Wimborne
2000	20/21 Art Fair, Royal College of Art, London
	Cadogan Contemporary Art

(forthcoming) 'Quiet Waters', Study Gallery, Poole with Peter Joyce, Prunella Clough, John Tunnard & Jeremy Gardiner

Collections (include)

TSB Group
National Westminster Bank
Reuters
Binder Hamlyn
Bank of China
Hill Samuel
Cleveland County Fine Art Collection
Russell Cotes Museum & Art Gallery
Poole Museum

ALEX LOWERY

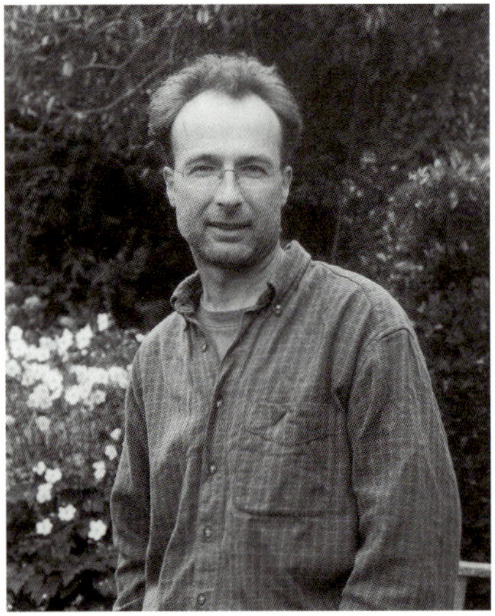

Since 1992, the almost exclusive subject of Alex Lowery's painting has been West Bay, a small settlement which lies about a mile and a half south of Bridport. It is perhaps the oldest and most historic port of Dorset and is both an ordinary and extra-ordinary place. It is here that the River Britt reaches the coast. Hatches regulate its flow into the harbour before the water is channelled between concrete piers and pushed out to sea. For the local people it has been a continual battle to prevent silt and shingle from closing the port. In recent years massive quarried boulders have been imported; they have been placed along the harbour entrance to help deflect the worst of winter storms. The beach itself, at West Bay, is shingle; it brings to an end a fourteen-mile coastal stretch known as the Chesil Bank, which originally starts in the vicinity of the Isle of Portland. At either end of the beach there are yellow sandstone cliffs. All have suffered degrees of erosion, yet on top of West Cliff there is an arrangement of houses and underneath a pedestrian walk.

At West Bay there is a sense of exposure and confrontation: the sea, the place and the people somehow not at ease with each other. As Lowery rightly says: "West Bay is very much willed into existence, it almost shouldn't be there, it's been imposed on the land." Overall, the place has a

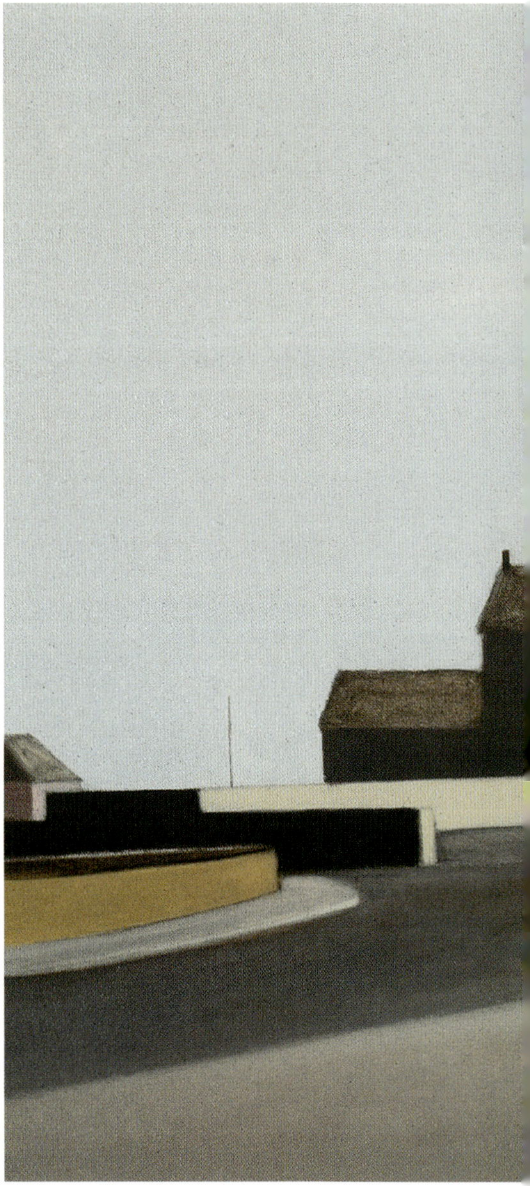

West Bay No. 148 (2000)

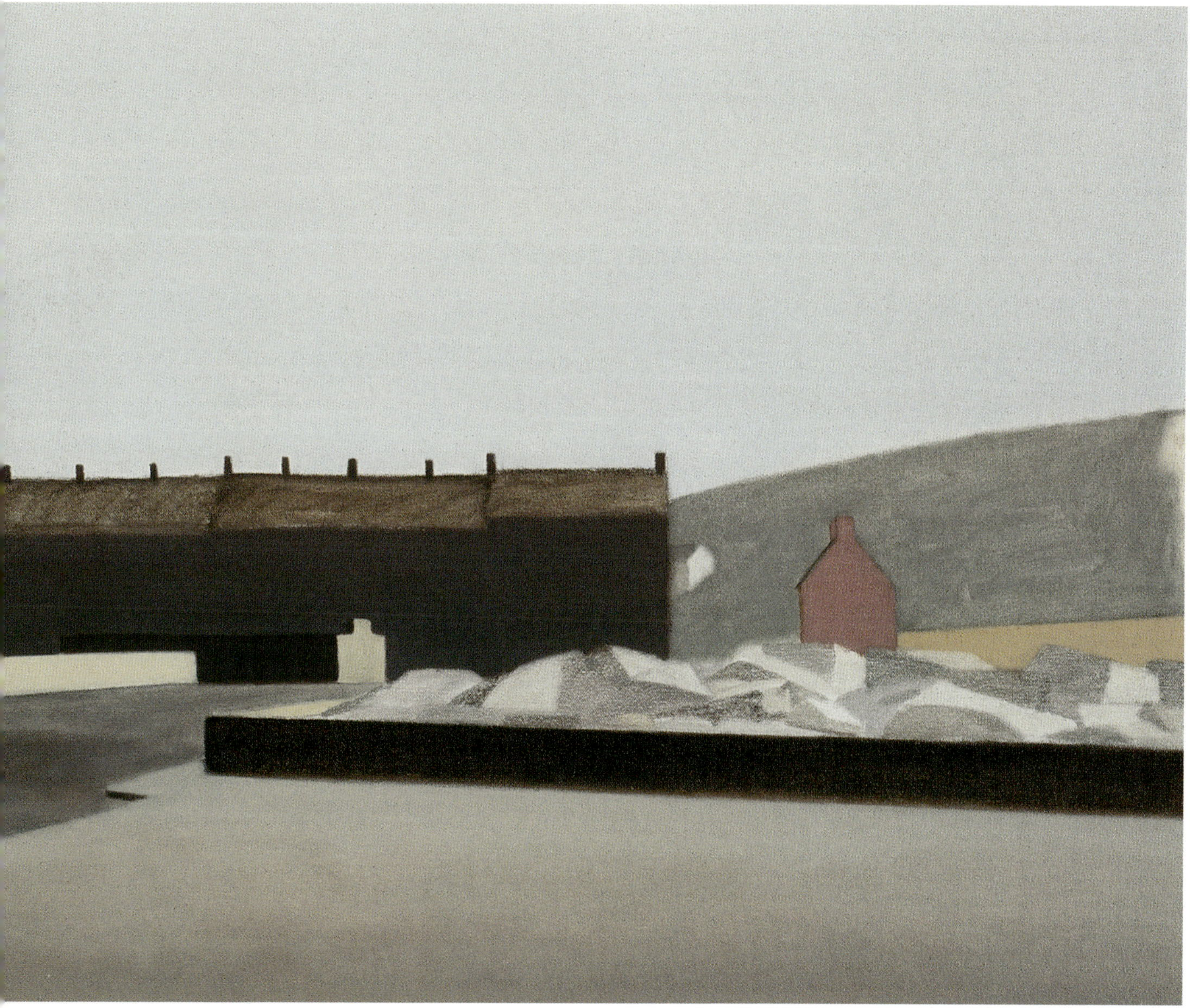

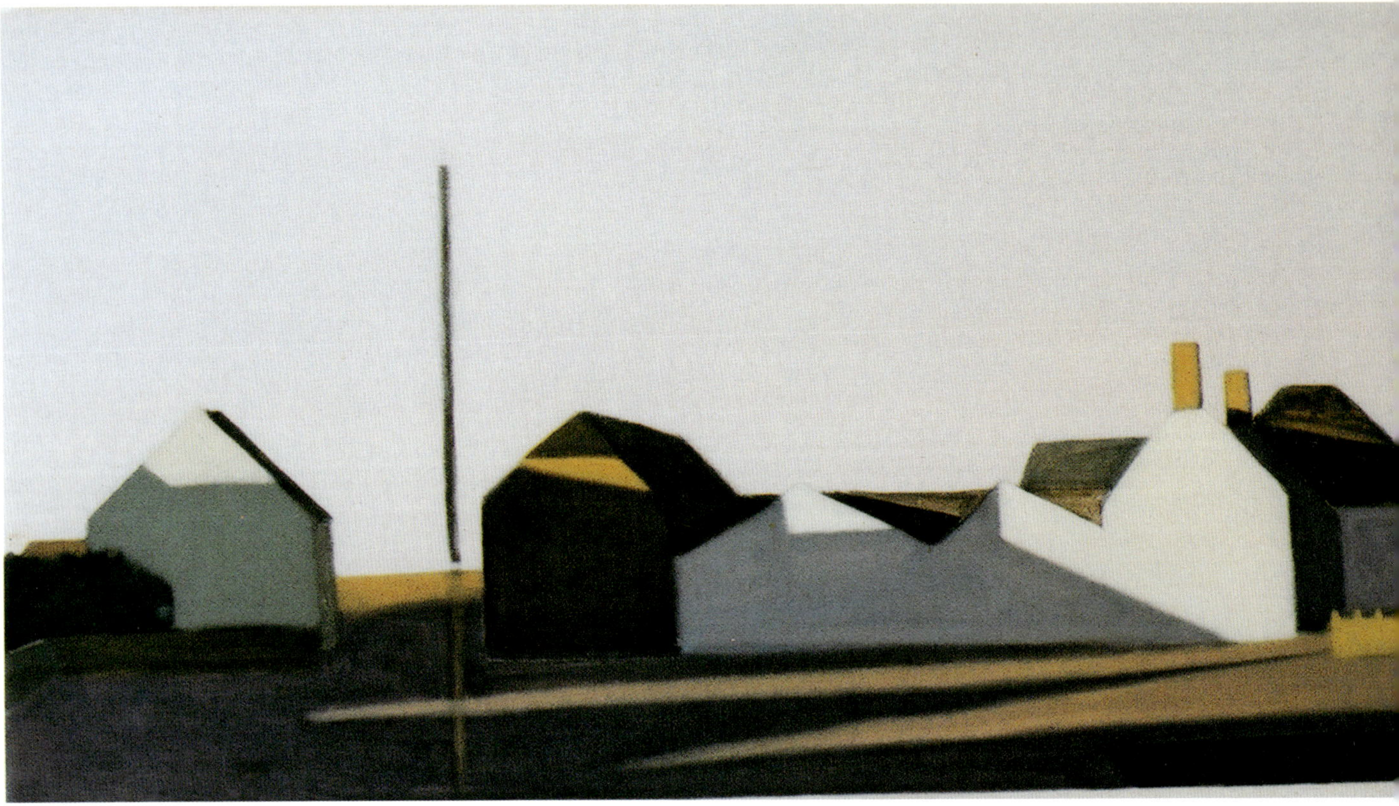

West Bay 116 (2000)

general sense of disharmony yet it retains the means to attract. There is a mix of old stone cottages and new bungalows, holiday chalets and wooden vending-booths. Dominating the harbour is E.S. Prior's tall four-storey block of houses known as Pier Terrace; impressive but out of synchrony with its neighbours (*West Bay 148*, 2000). In 1927, Maxwell described West Bay as a small place which did not know whether it was a village or a seaside resort. This indecisive status still seems to exist. As Lowery has observed, "there is that funny juxtaposition: it's got quite a suburban landscape, an odd little world and yet also it has this elemental thing - the sea - cheek by jowl."

For Lowery, West Bay's uniqueness is the presence of the sea. "You can't necessarily see it, but you know it's there. Indeed, its not being seen can actually increase your sense of its presence." On the east side of the harbour thatched cottages stand on the shingle, isolated like beached whales. Around them "the artificially raked beach is a barrier against the houses being swept away, houses built as it were on sand - demonstrating the vulnerability of the human aspect of the land."

Before Lowery began painting at West Bay he had been searching for some time for a new subject; a subject which in its very constraint and restriction would put an emphasis on invention. He wanted a constant against which to measure his work. Limiting himself to work with one subject he feels "helps to push forward the formal issues of painting. How are you going to treat the same buildings, cliff or harbour without just doing the same painting all the time?"

Lowery was born in London. At school, the Art Room was a place of escape where he could lose himself in an 'imaginative world'. Although deemed by his teacher to be good at drawing, colour had the stronger appeal. He speculates that becoming short sighted as a young child led him to see a world in which colour was a dominant force. He found that his first pair of glasses brought an unnerving clarity and focus of line and texture. Perhaps unsurprisingly, it was painters such as Matisse, Derain and Marquet who appealed to him as a young student at the Central School of Art (1979-82). He was particularly impressed by the way in which these painters made colour serve their art. Lowery has always had a 'sense of painting' which Merlin James (1995) described as having 'an ability to make subtle yet sure distinctions and value judgements while recognising that the nature and stature of past paintings remain open to appraisal, in the light ... of what painting does next.'[13] Today, Lowery still very much looks to past masters for the formal side of painting; to painters such as Piero della Francesca, Vermeer and Corot. Having assimilated these, however, he recognises "there comes a moment when you are alone; you must ride without stabilisers and create your own vision, language and style".

While at the Central School, Lowery's tutor, Garth Lewis, encouraged him to look at artists he had not previously been aware of while also "planting ideas which have helped my progress". Garth Lewis had been in America for some time and become familiar with the work of East Coast painters such as Fairfield Porter, Alex Katz, Richard Diebenkorn and Edward Hopper. "The work they were doing showed a new slant on potential directions for painting figuratively; a freshness, very un-English in a way, especially with regards to light." Porter, for example, painting in Maine's wide, open coastlands, captured the most subtle nuances of light, suggesting 'the very air around things by the use of colour alone' (Hughes,1997).[14]

The power to evoke the very breath and atmosphere of a place through the medium of colour has come to be one of Lowery's strengths. His paintings are about real light at real times of day, seen through the 'prism' of painting. Sometimes skies are blue while at other times they are of refracted and reflected colours: lilac, mint green and white. A preferred light of Lowery's is that of "fairly direct sun, usually quite clear, when you get that extra bounce of light from the sea". At other times there may be "a more milky or pearly quality which lends an emotional feel to the shadows". Cast shadow is an

West Bay I(1998)

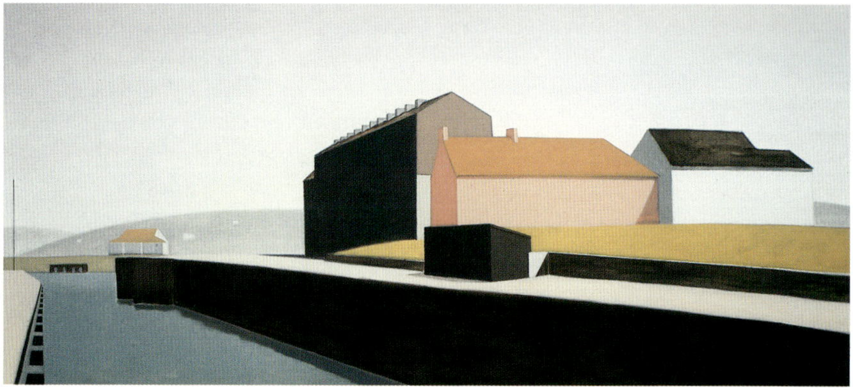

important compositional element of Lowery's work, as seen, for example, in *West Bay 116* (2000). Strong or soft edged shadows darken the ground and sides of buildings: they are the arena in which the interplay of light and space is revealed.

Lowery's earlier West Bay paintings were more inclusive of detail. In recent years, this detail has disappeared; it has become implicit rather than actual. There are no longer any cars in the streets or windows and doors in houses. Boat masts are reduced to minimal lines and houses to planed shapes. "Chimneys might be enough of a level of detail, for example, to imply everything else that exists at that level without having to spell it out. It is a kind of abstraction, although I can't currently imagine doing fully abstract work. I'm interested in where the abstract and non-abstract meet and overlap."

Lowery has always maintained that painting continues to be a valid medium in the world of contemporary art, although it has often been declared redundant. He acknowledges that painters working in the sphere of more 'traditional' art have tended to miss out on critical attention at the expense of those engaged in radical experimentation or in using the new technologies. Good art, he argues, is so much more than the fashion of the time. However, this is not to deny that, like other painters, he has occasional crises about the 'validity' of, for example, working with landscape. "Sometimes it's as if the curators, critics or collectors are setting the path, and this to me is the wrong way around." Although not against new media, he feels that the emphasis should be more on the quality of a piece than on the means of its realization.

In terms of setting about making work, Lowery finds it necessary to continue to draw and to take photographs at West Bay. Initially, he used to spend time there every week; now, there might be an interval of several weeks between visits. "At first I panicked about missing things, now the painting takes on its own momentum. One of the gains from

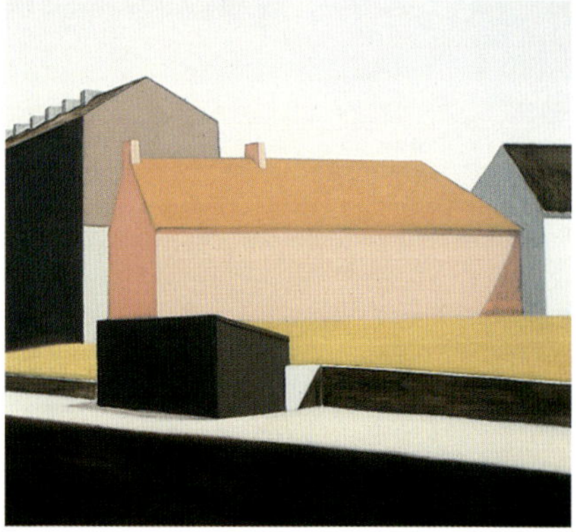

Detail *West Bay I*(1998)

having worked there so long is that I have a good mental idea of it and so can draw on several resources to create new work."

When Lowery begins a painting he will map out the composition with a fairly accurate charcoal drawing. As well as indicating structure, the charcoal also adds a tonal element, some of which he tries to retain to the end, although this is not always possible. Lowery always paints in oil, usually on a relatively fine-weave canvas. The painted surface plays an important role, and the fact that his brushstrokes are usually restrained rather than gestural underlines rather than diminishes this importance. Paint is applied thinly; this allows transparent, textural qualities to emerge. Tone and colour shifts vary from the smooth and seamless to the dramatic and bold. For many years Lowery used a restricted palette of about six colours. On his studio walls there are paint swatches of experimental colour mixes. Over the last years these colours have become paler, although he dismisses a 'sorbet' analogy as implying an overly saccharine quality. While working on a painting, Lowery feels his way ahead instinctively. Initially, colour comes from observed fact, but later the painting just takes off. "You start using the colours within the picture to balance other colours which may or may not be that close to reality."

Lowery believes that his paintings never quite enter a world "of overtly surreal, dream-like existentialism", but they can evoke sensations of unquiet events taking place just beyond our perception. The absence of door and window openings in buildings, of deep pier shadows reaching out to sea are unsettling images and do contribute to feelings of unease. On the other hand, the paintings do not seriously threaten. There is an openness in the sky and a luminosity in the light which surrounds the houses, harbour and cliffs. These softer, elemental qualities detach Lowery's houses and structures from their too-solid footings and place them in a lighter, more insubstantial plane and level of time.

Lowery is a painter who is, perhaps unfashionably, engaged with how formal issues interact with artistic meaning and expression. "Colour, light, space, balance - it's like harmonic progressions to a composer." The music analogy is in fact quite apt, as Lowery is a dedicated pianist who acknowledges that music does have a bearing on his painting. He particularly enjoys playing Haydn piano sonatas, which "exploit formal expectations and use them against the listener". Perhaps, not co-incidentally, this can equally be said of a Lowery painting.

In paintings of discipline and economy, Lowery opposes tension and formalism with insubstantial reality; atmospheric light with solid objectivity. His overall concern is with "the retinal thrill of the light, with what's hidden and what's revealed, with the essence of the place". With West Bay he has found a location he can work with, and his paintings exemplify the aphorism that less equals more.

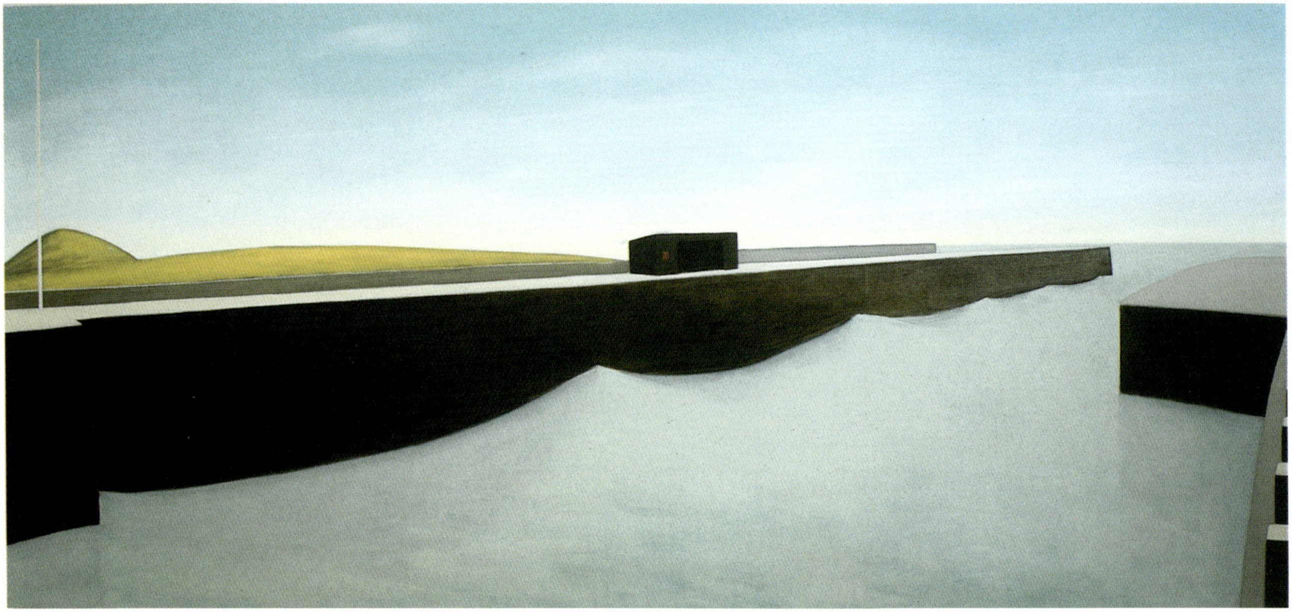

West Bay II (1998)

Biography

1957	Born London
1976-1977	Bath Academy of Art: Foundation Course
1978-1979	Sir John Cass School of Art, London
1979-1982	Central School of Art, London BA (Hons) Fine Art
1998	Major comminssion for Dorset County Hospital Phase II
1998	South West Arts – Major Financial Award
2000	Represented by Art First, London

Selected Solo Exhibitions

1993	Gordon Hepworth Gallery, Exeter
1994	County Museum, West Bay, Dorset
1995	Rocket Gallery, Cork Street, London
1997	Allsop Gallery, Bridport, Dorset
2000	Art First, Cork Street, London
2001	Bridport Arts Centre, Dorset
2002	Forthcoming: Art First, Cork Street, London

Selected Group Exhibitions

1993	Boundary Gallery, London
1994	Royal College, London
1995	Six Chapel Road Gallery, Bath
1995	Art 95, Business Design Art Centre, London
1995	Rocket Gallery, London
1996	Dusseldorf, Germany
1996-1997	Kettle's Yard, Cambridge
1997	Connaught Brown Gallery, London
1998	Piccadilly Gallery, London
1998	Gordon Hepworth, Cork Street, London
1999	Dorset County Hospital, Dorchester
1999	Art 99, Business Design Centre
2000	Art First, London
2001	Sherborne House, Dorset
2001	Art First, London

Literature

1995	'What's On' review by Andrew Lambirth (illustrated)
1995	'Art Review' Painting reproduced
1995	'London Magazine; Article by Merlin James
1995	'Remaking Reality' Catalogue essay by Simon Wallis
1996	'Modern Painters' Review by David Cohen (illustrated)
1999	'Art Review' Mike Lambert (illustrated)
1999	Catalogue for Bournemouth University

PÁDRAIG MACMIADHACHÁIN

I want a room big enough to love in
work in
and sometimes eat in

from its window
I must see the sea
feel the wind outside

I want a room above the houses
to sleep in
when the streets are tired with people
and I am tired with talking

The address is not important
But the shutters must be blue

Pádraig Macmiadhháchin
From *The Secret Door*, 1977[15]

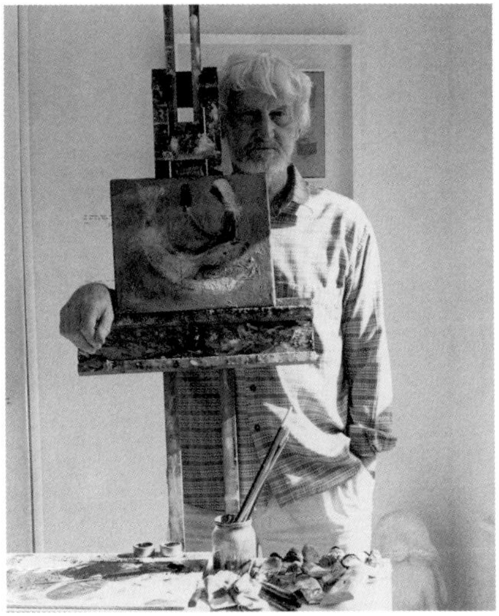

Pádraig Macmiadhháchin lived the early part of his life in Downpatrick, Northern Ireland, but at the age of twenty-four he moved to Swanage in Dorset. This seaside town of Purbeck sits sheltered in the lee of Ballard Down. Once it was the centre for the Purbeck Stone trade. Massive blocks of Purbeck Stone and Marble were cut and blasted from local quarries before being transported, by rail and road, to moored ships at Swanage quay. In the 1800s, two entrepreneurs, George Burt and his uncle, John Mowlem, transformed the town into a Victorian seaside resort. From London they brought re-claimed masonry facades including cast-iron columns and an archway from Hyde Park Corner. Durlston Castle (1890), was built as a restaurant; and a Great Globe, with a diameter of twelve feet, was sculpted in London and brought to Swanage. Burt and Mowlem also installed the town's first pumped water system. In effect, they placed the seaside town of Swanage firmly on the tourist map and there it has stayed ever since.

In summer the population swells by thousands and in winter shrinks back again. Hyland (1978), wrote that Swanage was the craziest town he knew, having: 'the sublimity of long history, the charm of a fishing village, the ambition and pragmatism of a port and the

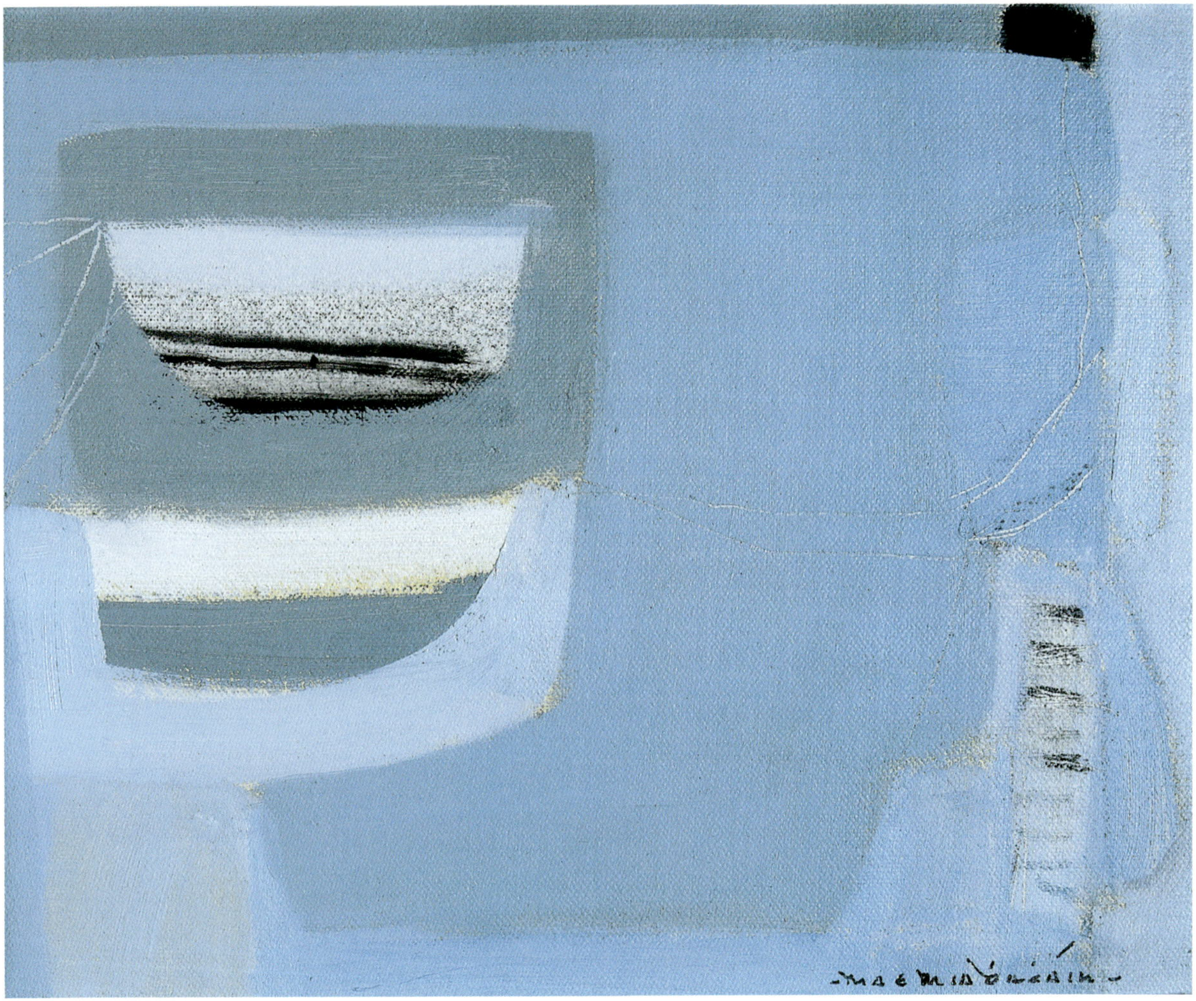

Paddy's Boat (2001)

calculated grace of a watering place'[16]. However, Macmiadháchin enjoys the anomalies and inherent contradictions of the place. His view is that Swanage is an unpretentious place and although the many local shopkeepers "may gossip like the clappers" they are very friendly.

Macmiadháchin is married to Jane, who is also a painter, and their home is Wharf House Studio, Commercial Lane. It is the last house of an old stone terrace, with a low-walled front garden and small back-yard. The Lane is a narrow but busy pedestrian thoroughfare right in the heart of the town. The front door is nearly always open and the invited entrance fee is a fifteen pence donation to the Lifeboat Fund. In studio rooms, both upstairs and down, oil paintings hang in close ranks and are even stacked against each other on the floor. There is a relentless energy in their number. For Macmiadháchin painting is a compulsion: even if he didn't sell anything he would still carry on.

The restlessness of the house is compounded by the walls and surfaces of every room being confettied with both acquired and found objects: early Spanish tiles, toys, model boats, fishing floats, photographs, tools and artefacts. It is an inclusive kaleidoscopic collection of the domestic to the archival, the naïve to the ornate. They are a presence in themselves; an exciting overdose of colour, shape and pattern.

Keeping them company are the sculptures and paintings which Macmiadháchin has bought over the years. Most are works by artists who have an association with the West Country, particularly St. Ives: artists such as Hilton, Wallis, Scott, Heron and McClure. Macmiadháchin particularly admires Hilton and his freedom and ability to work 'completely abstract'. It is no easy task to achieve a successful composition without a figurative scaffolding. It involves "getting everything in the right place". Such an undertaking lies at the heart of Macmiadháchin's painting.

Initially Macmiadháchin trained in Fine Art at Belfast College of Art (1947-1949) where his time was spent "purely drawing ... academic training". He then studied portrait painting under Sean Keating at the National College of Art, Dublin (1950). In 1960 he won a Polish Government Scholarship to the Academy of Fine Art, Kracow, Poland. It was here that he first came upon the work of Piotr Potworowski, who was a Polish landscape painter who also had links with painters in St. Ives, Cornwall. Macmiadháchin admired Potworowski's "natural feeling for the landscape, the way he abstracted it and his gorgeous colour and texture". It encouraged him to work less with the human figure and more with "the landscape or whatever I was standing in front of". In time, Macmiadháchin's own paintings became more abstract. "Now I move in and out of abstraction, some are more figurative than others. I don't give myself any hard and fast rules or regulations."

Fishing Lines (2001)

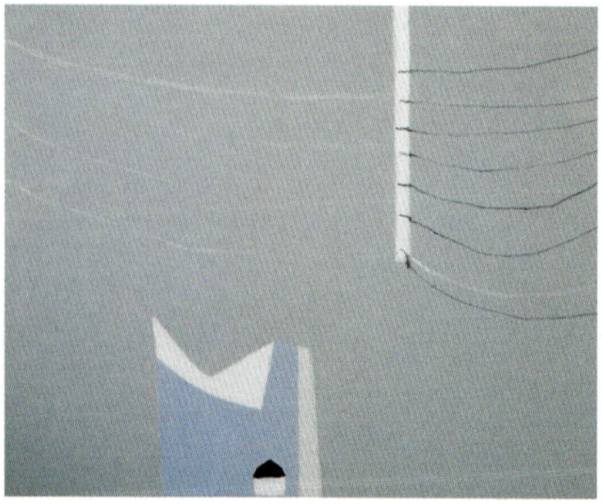

Certainly Macmiadhcháin is not afraid to shift between fantasy and narrative or figurative and abstract. He is also happy to work with colours which range from the riotous to the subdued. Although the main body of his work remains centred on the coastal landscape and harbours of Purbeck and Cornwall, Macmiadhcháin has occasional, unexpected 'outbursts' of other subjects. The *Argentine Ice Cream* series originated from four visits, over six years, to Argentina. He has written (Arts Loan Catalogue, 2000)[17] that they record the 'vitality and buzz of Buenos Aires and the colours of Argentine ice cream'. They are joyful, celebratory, textural abstract works. In contrast, the Spanish *La Guardia Civil* paintings are figurative, and although not sombre in colour or tone, are disturbing and unsettling in mood and composition (*The Bride and Groom,* 2000). Cloaked guards wear 'shovel'hats and hide behind dark, opaque glasses. They stand next to civilians and emanate a 'threatening' air although their responsibility is to protect the vulnerable. Usually there is a moon or sun in the sky but the sea is as likely to be green as blue and the sand, pink as yellow. Such colour choices, Macmiadháchin argues, stems from true observation: "October in Gozo the sea is blue with pinks and orange while ... December in Uruguay, greens are everywhere and a blue colour arises over everything."

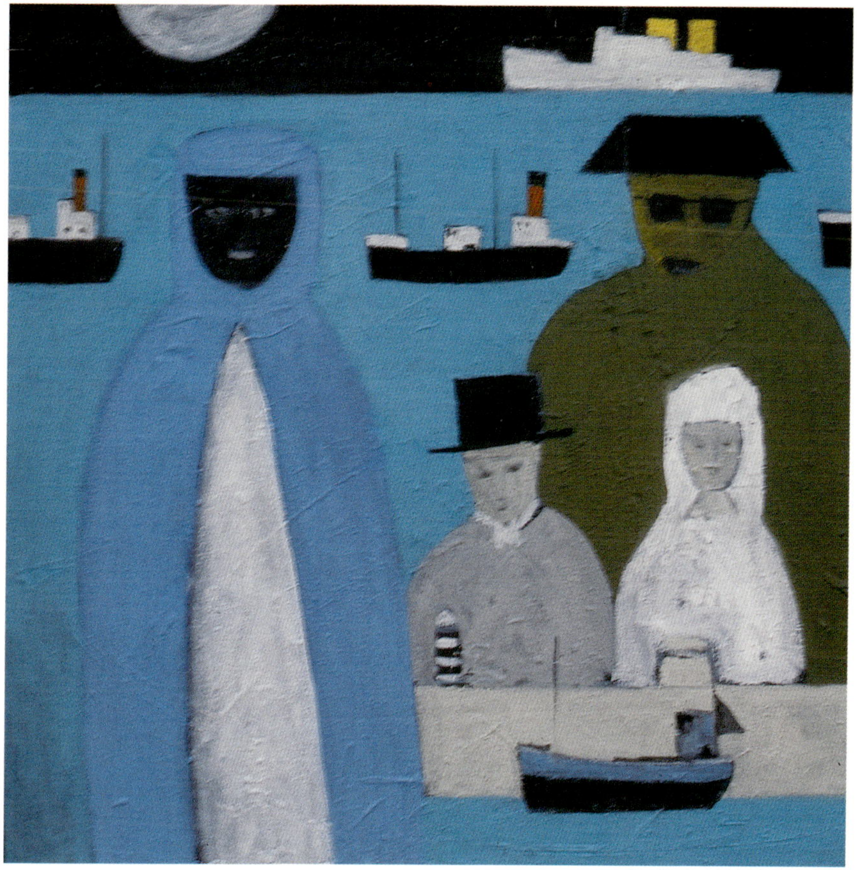

The Bride and Groom (2000)

For over forty years Macmiadháchin has painted full-time. For the first eighteen months after leaving College he supported his painting by working at a youth hostel at Killeyneather Castle, County Down. When the hostel closed it was an ex-college friend who suggested he came to Swanage. Here he found work in the kitchens of an hotel in Studland. He met a local painter and teacher from Corfe Castle by the name of Edgar Milward and together they rented The Old Mill in Swanage. "I came back from work about two o'clock every day and we went down to the Mill and opened up, painted and sold pictures. We had tilley lamps for light at night because there was no electricity."

By the end of the first summer, Macmiadháchin had saved enough money to go and spend the winter in Ibiza. "There was no airport on Ibiza in those days, there was only a boat once a week to Barcelona. There were about twenty foreigners living on the island, quite a few painters. Stayed all winter and then came back in the spring, no money again so had to go back to the hotel and do another season." However, that was the last time, except for one separate occasion, when Macmiadháchin worked at anything other than painting. "You don't need a lot of money if you live in Swanage. It's not an expensive place. Most of the things I enjoy, like walking, swimming and mooching around the beach, don't cost anything."

Since this first winter trip abroad, Macmiadhàchin has made winter travel a regular fixture. "For about twenty years I used to go to the Canary Islands. In those days you could get a passage on liners from Southampton, going to Cape Town or Montevideo or wherever. A week before they sailed if they hadn't filled up every berth on the ship they'd sell them off to those going to the Canaries. So, we'd take the train to Southampton, get off and take the liner, just close everything and disappear. It didn't cost any more than staying here because it was very cheap to travel and the cost of living there was very inexpensive. Also, there was so much more daylight for working so I painted down there. When you're travelling by sea, you can bring an enormous amount of baggage. I'd bring lots of canvasses back, you couldn't do that on air planes now."

His more recent visits have been to a friend's three hundred year-old farmhouse on the Mediterranean Island of Gozo, and to Uruguay and Argentina. Time away from Purbeck is important. "It's not so much going away to look at something else, though that's exciting, but when I come back I see things I've been looking at for years in a new way. I love coming back and I love going away."

Macmiadhàchin paints intuitively. "Everything goes in through my eyes. It's visual first, probably colour and then the feel of whatever I'm looking at." For Macmiadhàchin, Purbeck is a very special place, and, in particular, the headland of St. Aldhelm's, which can be fiercely wild. On summer days, however: "you can feel the warmth of the sun on your skin and through to your bones. It's a spiritual quality up there. It's a place I go to and regenerate ...... when somebody's rattled my cage. I'll walk out from Renscombe Farm, out towards the Headland ... I must have walked it hundreds and hundreds of times. Jane, my wife, described it once as a place where you feel so near the sky ... there's that flat feel up there, you're above everything."

On the top of the Headland there is a squat, square, Norman chapel. It stands a hundred and eight metres above sea level and is close to a Coastguard look-out station and some Coastguard cottages. The Chapel is lit by a single, narrow, deep window which is filled with new stained glass. "There's a lovely feeling in the Chapel, it's beautiful, it's peaceful. Around the Chapel you can make out a ridge, it's very close to the Chapel and is now designated 'An Early Christian Enclosure'. No wonder! I've always found peace here." Macmiadhàchin has painted the Chapel innumerable times. So much so that one elderly Swanage resident on seeing a 'new' Chapel painting, commented: "He's always painting that Chapel up at St. Aldhelm's Head. He's painted it hundreds of times. I'm sure he'll get it right yet!"

Close to St. Aldhelm's is the footpath from Winspit to the village of Worth Matravers. Here on the hillside there are strip-lynchets, a tracery terrace once worked by medieval farmers. In winter when the sun is low "they're like ribs, the bones of a landscape".

Macmiadháchin has often depicted their linear shapes in his oil paintings, drawing them in with charcoal. They break the natural shape of the land and offer themselves as ready-made marks to be used.

Macmiadháchin enjoys working with charcoal. On the occasions when he uses acrylics, as when travelling, he will mix in the charcoal, or something similar, to take the sheen off the paint. He likes the sound charcoal makes on paper and it is always his tool for sketching. "I'll often take a sketchbook out. I never use the sketches; very rarely. Once you sit down and actually observe, put down what you're looking at, it sticks in your mind or parts of it will."

When painting in his Studio, Macmiadháchin often works until midnight and always plays music. "My favourite music for working to is Techno. I love that beat, I get lost in it." However, he also plays a selection of other music which ranges from Modern Jazz to Shostakovich. "My taste is very catholic. Music forms like a cocoon around my head and I'm in the middle of it and therefore nothing else gets in, so there's just me and the canvas and I'm surrounded by music."

Apart from occasional outbursts into bright colour, Macmiadháchin remains fairly constant to the 'natural' colours of the Purbeck coast. In these coastal paintings he is at his most serene: oil is applied in smooth satin layers. The paintings possess a tranquillity which truly reflects Macmiadháchin's feelings about the place: "the tremendous green in the fields, the beautiful blue triangle of sea glimpsed when walking, the white cliffs halfway between Haysom's Quarry and St. Aldhelm's Head and the grey stone walls and lichened bushes that grow up around them".

Pale Bay (2001)

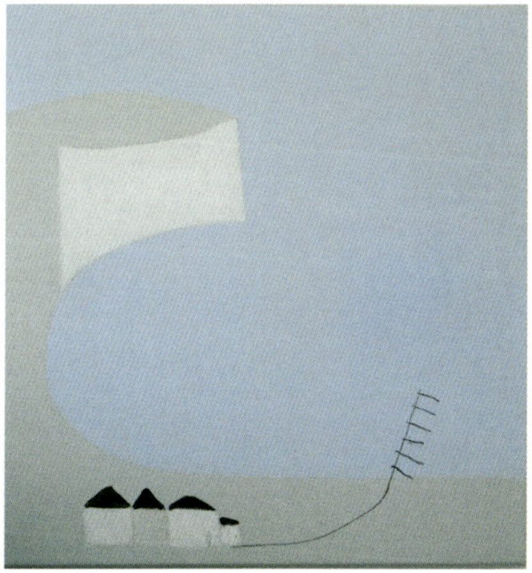

It is in his bay paintings, such as *Pale Bay* (2001), that Macmiadháchin is at his most minimal. However, the calm surfaces, limited colours, shapes and lines that make up these paintings do not make for an easier life. In fact, he believes the reverse is true, as 'the less detail you have in a picture the more you have to ensure that each piece is perfect in its own right and in relation to the other elements' (Macmiadháchin, 1999)[18].

White is an important colour for Macmiadháchin and he uses it a lot. "Some of my paintings are nearly all white with just a few marks on but there are occasions when I like working with what I call muddy colours; the colours that the German Army used on their vehicles in the last War. You find them all around you on the stones, lichens and cliffs. When they've just quarried some of the Purbeck Stone it comes out a pale yellow colour and as it mellows it turns lovely greys. Then there are the blacks. There's a very warm black you find on the roofs of buildings around lighthouses. Trinity House buildings always have tarred roofs. There's that gleam of white ...... I love lighthouses ...... There's one up at Anvil Point, but it's not so much the lighthouse up there but the

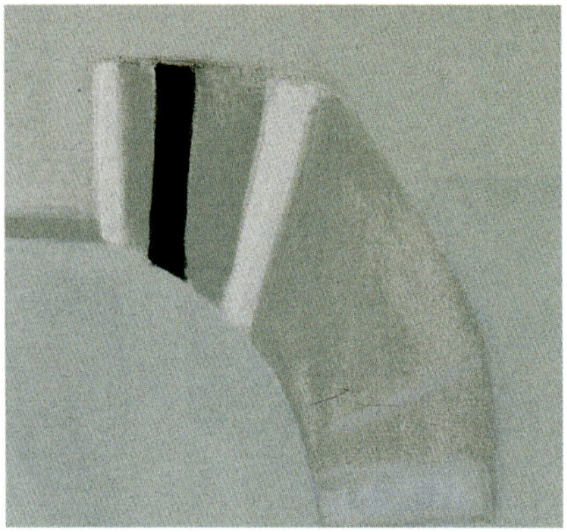

Detail *Jack Pender's Harbour* (2000)

collection of seven little buildings behind it. They used to keep equipment for cliff rescue there." At Peveril Point there are six Coastguard cottages against the beach which have black chimneys with five or six black pots on them.

Accompanying a love of coastal buildings is his love of boats (*Paddy's Boat,* 2001) and all things to do with boats (*Fishing Lines,* 2001). "I've thought about it and I wondered why I love fishing boats. My earliest childhood memory would have been somewhere around the age of four, when I was living in Downpatrick with my parents and they used to rent a little house in a little fishing village called Ardglass. I used to love walking down on the quay when all the herring gutting girls were there and all the fish and the fabulous smells, it stayed with me ever since. I love that smell you get in a fishing port, it can be a bit rotten at times but I like it ...... old tarred ropes. I collect the old glass floats that they used to use, they're beautiful. They used to use them for holding up nets; all plastic ones now."

Jack Pender's Harbour (2000)

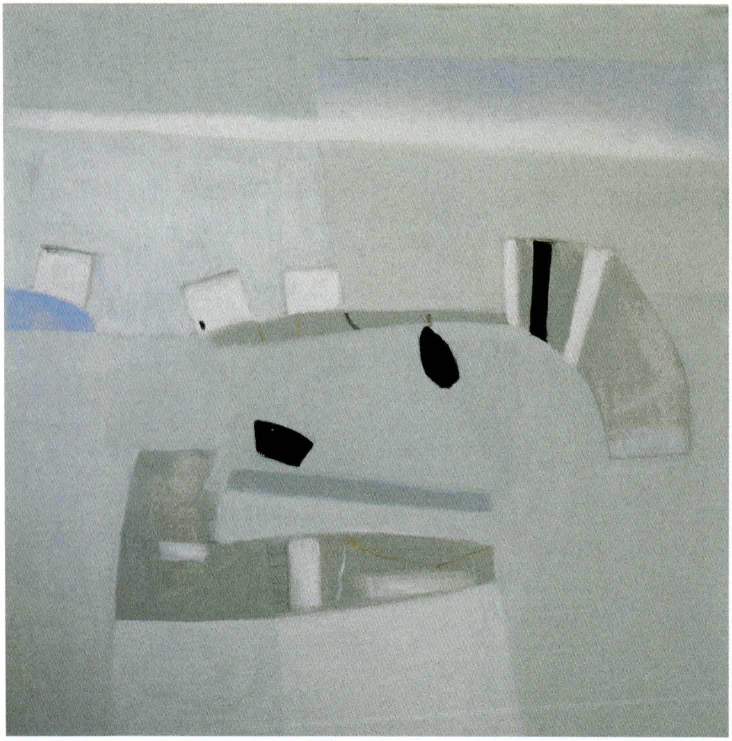

Macmiadhháchin believes he has always loved fishing boats and the colours of them, "the boats that come from Scotland particularly. They're very often painted black with bits of blue and white: these are colours that I like. Usually we go down to St. Ives for about three months in the winter. This is where we've been going instead of the Canaries. The place we rent is an old sail loft, done up now like a little holiday flat, it's overlooking the harbour (*Jack Pender's Harbour,* 2000). I like just sitting at the window and watching all the activity. If I'm down there it's not landscape I'm painting it's vague shapes of boats. Painters and fishermen have one world down there."

Whatever Macmiadhháchin does, is done because he wishes to do it and for no other reason than that. Written over his kitchen door he has inscribed 'I'm allowed to be me'. He both needs and enjoys time away, but his roots, after over forty years, are definitely fixed in Purbeck. In painting the landscape he "can walk through it, enjoy it and feel how beautiful it is day after day" - while aiming always to 'get things in the right place'

Biography

1929 Born Downpatrick, Ireland
1947-49 Belfast College of Art
1950 National College of Art, Dublin
1957 Moscow Scholarship, sponsored by Soviet Government
1960 Polish Scholarship, sponsored by the British Council
1991 Winner LAING National Painting Competition
1992 Winner Daler-Rowney Award
1993 Winner LAING Regional Painting Competition
Associate member: Penwith Society of Arts, St Ives

Collections Include:

A.I.B
The Arts Council of Ireland
HM Juan Carlos, King of Spain
Lord Briggs
Sir Michael Culme-Seymour
Ronald Alley, former Head of Modern British Painting, Tate, London
The late Peter Sellars
Bob Monkhouse
NBC
Caja Insular de Ahorres de Gran Canaria
Escuela de Bellas Artes (Las Palmas)
Hertford College, Oxford
Sussex University
The late President Chenyenkov, Soviet Union
The Bank of China
S. G. Warburg
Sun Oil International
Toshby Investments (Japan)
Daido Insurance (Japan)
Kobe Steel
West Merchant Bank
John and Jennie Makepeace

Selected One/Two/Three Man Exhibitions

1951-52 Donegall Place Gallery, Belfast
1953 Capitol Theatre Gallery, Dublin
1955 Instituto de Cultura Hispanica, Madrid
1956 Robinson and Cleaver Gallery, Belfast
1957 New Vision Gallery, London
1958-1959 Woodstock Gallery, London
1960 Grabowski Gallery, Bournemouth
1960 Arts Council Gallery, Belfast
Lincoln Gallery, London
Akedemia Stuk Pieknych, Poland
Osiris Gallery, Oxford
Old Town Hall, Reigate, England
1967 Hambledon Gallery, Blandford, England
St Martin's Court Gallery, London
1970 Queen's University, Belfast
1971,1973 Liberty's Gallery, London
Nicholas Treadwell Gallery, London
London Gallery, Los Angeles, USA
1975-1976 Heals Gallery, London
1977 Yles Galena Las Palmas, Canary Islands
Century Galleries, Henley, England
Sala Cairasco, Las Palmas, Canary Islands
Canning House Gallery, London
Torrance Gallery, Seattle, USA
Griffiths Gallery West, Vancover, Canada
1984 Federation of Canadian Artists Gallery
Canning House Gallery, London
1987 Grove Arts Gallery, Dorchester
1987 Canning House Gallery, London
1990-00 New Academy Gallery, London (six exhibitions)
1993 Salt House Gallery, St Ives, England
1994 Kessler Gallery, Miami, USA
1997 New Millenium Gallery, St Ives, England
1999/2001 Molesworth Gallery, Dublin, Ireland
2000 'Fedden's Choice', Joint Exhibition, London

Forthcoming: 2002 New Academy Gallery, London

Selected Group Exhibitions

1969 Northern Young Contemporaries. Whitworth Art Gallery, Manchester.
Arts Council travelling exhibition
1976 First Artists from Cubertou Exhibition at Compton, Chichester
1979 FBA Galleries, Artists from Cubertou Cubertou Art Centre, France
1976-1980 Artists from Cubertou group shows in England
RA Summer Exhibitions
1990-94 Summerleaze Gallery
1995 Alpha House Gallery, Sherbourne
1995,1997 Royal West of England Academy
1995 A Blend of North Dorset, Salisbury Library
1996 Seldown Gallery, Poole Arts Centre
1997 Quantum Fine Art, London
1999 Richmond Hill Gallery, London
1999 Bettles Gallery, Ringwood
1999 Bournemouth University Art Loan Collection, Atrium Gallery
2000 Maltby Contemporary Art, Winchester

Selected Group Exhibitions

He has taken part in collective exhibitions of paintings: The Royal Acadamy of Arts, London; The Royal West of England Academy, Bristol; The Royal Ulster Academy, Belfast; Dublin, Paris, Moscow, Toronto and Miami.

ALASTAIR MICHIE

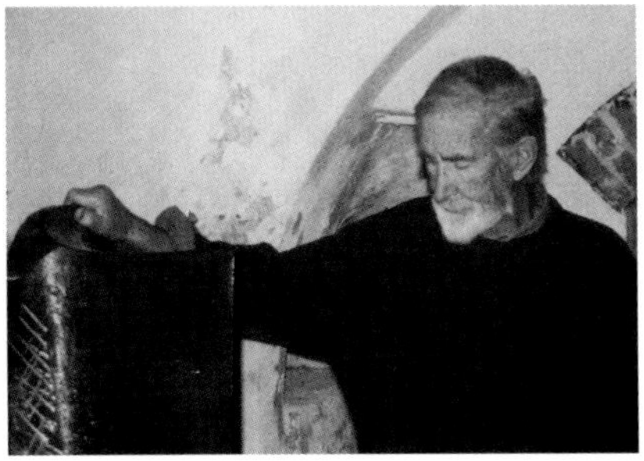

Somewhat hidden from the main street, behind thick glossy bay trees, there is an elegant Queen Anne house in South Street, Wareham. The house was built for Mr. George Gould, but two fires in the town have destroyed records that would have given the present residents, Alastair and Sally Michie, the full history of the house. Shadowed under the bay trees is a decorative metal gate, seemingly never quite closed. It opens to steps which rise to a front door with polished brass. Inside the house there is a long hall with paired side rooms. All is elegant, high and painted, yet the rooms, rather than succumbing to a cool classicism, spin out colour and warmth like an unravelling silk cocoon. It is a Venetian place of colour; deep and confident, vibrant and alive. Textiles, objects, dark wood, lit lamps, painted white panels, gilt and paintings everywhere. In such a place an evening fire, whether winter or summer, seems to be at ease with the spirit of the place.

Outside the house, the road leads south to Wareham Quay and the River Frome. Beyond lies a causeway which crosses treeless marshland to the hills of Purbeck. Wareham is an ancient town and many famous names are associated with the place; names such as T.E. Shaw (better known as Lawrence of Arabia); the young Saxon King Edward, who was murdered by his stepmother at Corfe Castle; and John Hutchins, who wrote an eighteenth-century *History of Dorset*.

Ralph Wightman, a Dorset farmer and author, observed that in spite of Wareham being swept by fire so often, the feeling of an 'abiding' place was very strong.[19] It is certainly a place where the painter and sculptor, Alastair Michie, has been happy to abide for over forty years. Yet, though he has lived all this time in Dorset, he has had an eventful life: full of unexpected swatches of colour, just like one of his paintings.

Michie was born (1921) in the north of France at St. Omer but moved when he was four years old to the South of France. He recounts: "My father was employed by an American millionaire called Thompson, who had invented the Thompson carburettor at a very useful time, as it was the beginning of the age of flight. My father was employed as a private architect and we settled in a village below the heights of Cap Ferrat. There were great estates above the village, the homes of such luminaries as Somerset Maugham. We were brought up in the grounds of a great château, the Château Gloria, and grew up like young French kids. But then came the Wall Street Crash. When that happened, my father's income stopped overnight. In the course of time we came back to Scotland, which was my father's and mother's home."

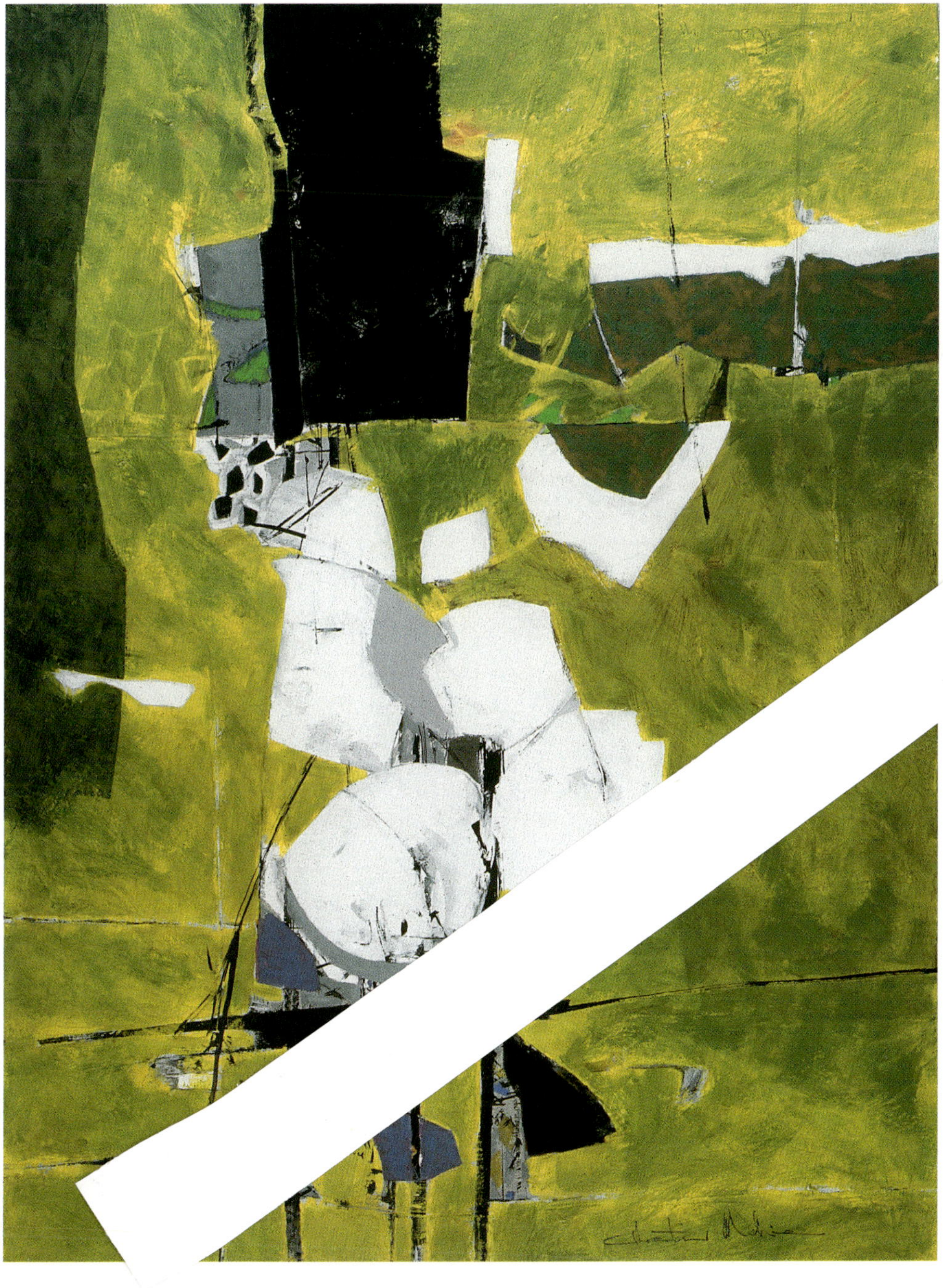

Transformer

Michie's mother, Anne Redpath [1899-1964], was the first woman to be elected a full Royal Scottish Academician. In her late paintings she distanced herself from the more figurative and began to use colour and texture for their own intrinsic qualities and effect. This work Michie likes best, the paintings "when she became more abandoned, colourful and wild, almost abstract". Although he acknowledges that his love of colour probably stems from his inheritance, he believes that even if he had not seen his mother's work "it's in the genes".

Alastair Michie did not go to art school. He is a self-taught painter and sculptor and very proud of it: "I remember once speaking to my mother. She'd seen some of my early work and I said: ' Do you think it possible for me to ever become a painter since I've had no academic training?' She said that it could be a handicap, and she left it at that". Instead of art school, Michie went to Edinburgh University to study architecture. However, with the onset of World War II he joined the RAF and became one of the youngest pilots to receive his wings. "I was a night fighter, an intruder. I flew one of the best-designed aircraft, a Mosquito, Rolls Royce twin engine. It was a fine aircraft, very fast and I enjoyed flying it enormously. Then eventually war came to an end and I found suddenly I'd survived and I thought what do I do now? The only thing I knew about at the age of twenty-four was flying."

Initially, he returned to Edinburgh University to continue his third year of architecture, but he couldn't settle to it: "I got completely bored because I wanted to get on with my life. I'd survived and I wanted to do things". He had always been a good draughtsman and quickly he established himself as a successful illustrator with International Artists and Artist Partners. It was a visit to the Venice Biennale, in 1962, which changed the direction of his life. "Never having taken a great interest in the world of painting I suddenly was electrified by seeing huge works by the American Abstract Expressionists such as Mark Rothko, Robert Motherwell and Franz Kline. I couldn't wait to get home and start painting and that's what I did." His first exhibition was at the Traverse Theatre, Edinburgh, in 1964, and he has been painting and exhibiting ever since.

Michie moved from Edinburgh to Dorset in 1950. He first lived with his family in a flat at Sandford House near Wareham. It was a fine turn-of-the-century house with about six acres of wonderful rhododendrons, conifers and azaleas. He felt very much at home there: "It was to do with the landscape which at first sight, the heathland, the conifers, the sandy soil, the look of the landscape was very much like Border country in Scotland. I liked the feel of it. That was the first thing; not a painterly thing as I was not then painting. But when I started to paint I became very aware of the Dorset landscape. The most dramatic impact was the discovery of the coastline; of places like Winspit and Seacombe. The Dorset coastline is infinitely varied and very powerful. With great split rocks at Winspit, and the caverns, there's a very graphic look to the landscape, like

Japanese calligraphy. That was the beginning, the biggest impact on my work ... the discovery of the architectural coastline ... Dancing Ledge and all these strange places."

The move to the Manor House at Wareham came five years after his initial move to Dorset. Today, the cellar of the house, once the original kitchen, is Michie's studio. Curved stairs lead down to a white barrel-vaulted room, which, after many years of 'battling with the damp', is now dry and well-lit. It is quiet here, isolated and immured from the sound of traffic; traffic which surprisingly moves along the road just metres away from the studio walls. Michie's sculptures, drawings, painting materials and photographs cover every working surface. Large canvasses stand on the floor, comfortably leaning against each other like familiar books on a shelf. Michie's Studio is a calm place and accords with a man who in both working and private life tends towards solitude.

He was once a great walker but no longer walks as he used to. For his painting this is not so crucial. He has never relied on sketches. "My work on the whole is really very abstract. I don't need to sit in front of a landscape in order to be fed. It's the way I work now." His resource is more a cumulative lifetime of images, experiences, colours and shapes, and the visual memories he draws on are wide-ranging. "Anything and everything will trigger the senses into applying the first brush-strokes on my canvas". One memory he has is of a flight in which the plane had to refuel at Recife. Circling the airfield before they landed, he became aware of the "extraordinary red colour of the soil". This observation was to be used later in many paintings. Michie remembers his time in Brazil (1972) as being both a powerful visual experience and an emotional one. He met many writers whilst he was there, including George Armado. He also exhibited at various galleries. The Museums of Modern Art at Sao Paolo and Rio de Janeiro both purchased some of his larger work.

Detail *The Last Lily*

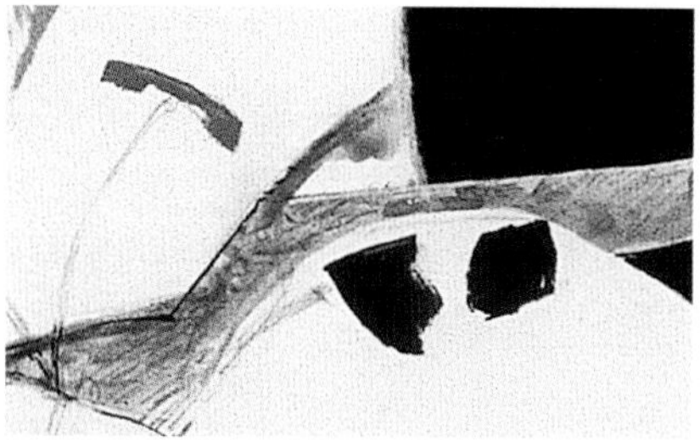

When Michie begins a composition, he first makes a tiny thumbnail plan of what he is going to do and then he starts to block in the shape. "Gradually I get there. You go on until you decide it's time to stop. You have to know when to stop and I think that's one of the most difficult things to do."

The Last Lily

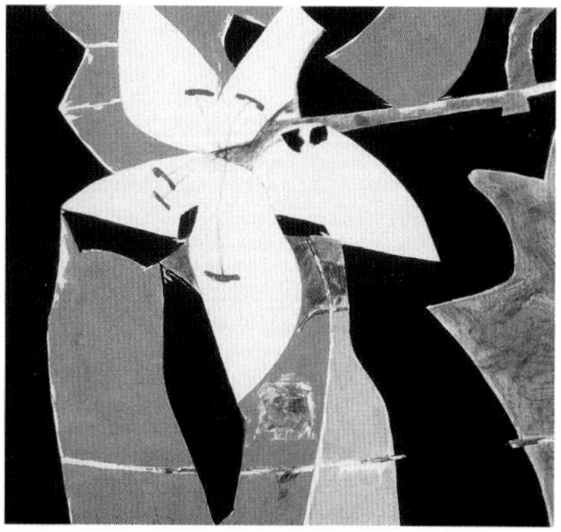

Sometimes, while completing a smaller work, he sees the way to a larger composition. This is the case with *The Last Lily* and *Margins*. In the lily painting the flower head is set against irregular, vertical bands (or margins), of either soft modulated greys, lilacs and whites or strong, uncompromising black. The *Lily* series was initially inspired by Michie having grown some enormous lilies; "they were spectacular, very white, very tall, waxy and heavily scented". Although these paintings are more figurative than most of his other work, there is still, with the emphasis on shape and flat areas of colour, a suggestion of abstraction from landscape.

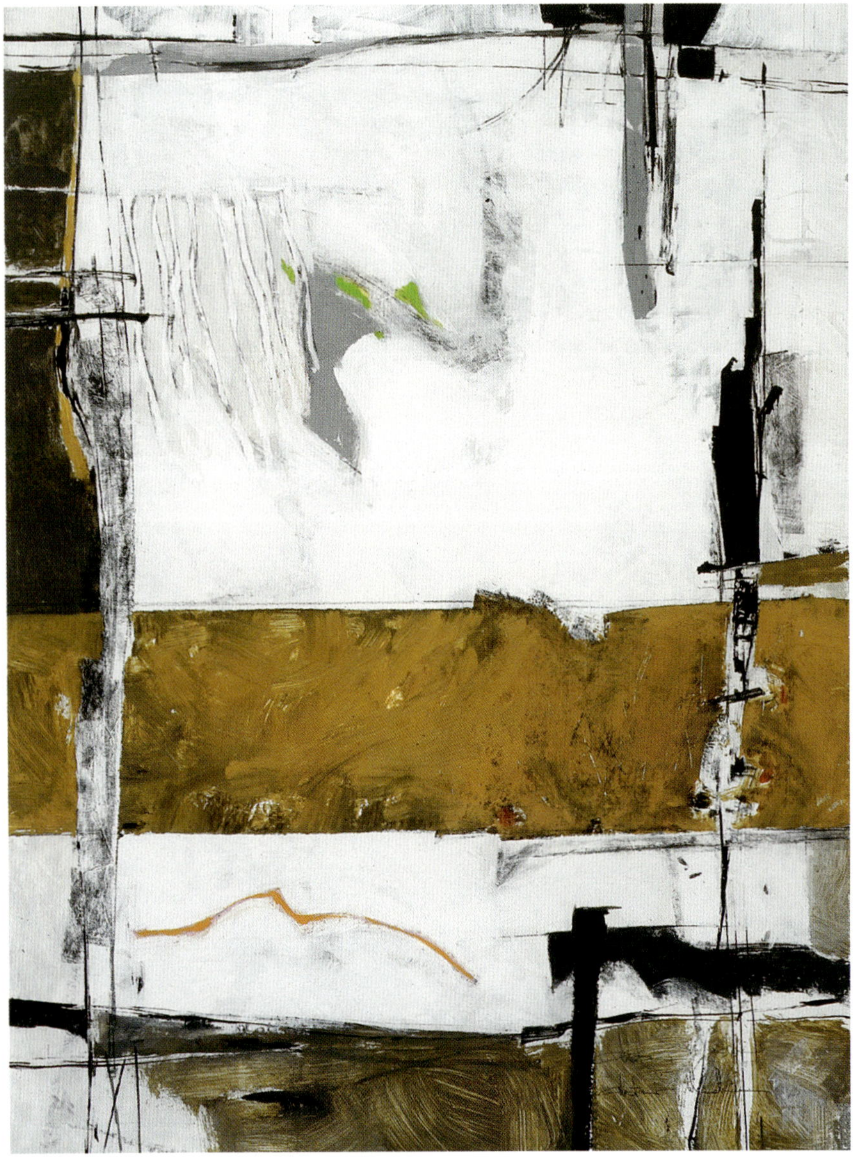

Margins

Michie's favourite canvas size is twenty-eight by thirty-six inches, (210mm x 915mm). He now paints almost entirely with acrylic, using it either as a body colour or thinly, like watercolour. Sometimes he introduces other media, particularly charcoal for drawn lines. Oil no longer suits his way of working. "I can attack with acrylic much better and at the end of the day, if I've had a session on a painting, I can put it in a frame under glass, take it upstairs, have a drink and walk around it and see what I can do the next time. I just like working with acrylic, it's quick drying. It suits my temperament, I work very quickly".

Michie has never worked in a formulaic manner. For him, each painting has the right to be different, to stand alone. However, in spite of this, there is something about a Michie painting that is distinctive and recognisable. His aim is always to achieve colour balance, composition and discipline.

Michie's use of paint has become less textural since he began sculpting. His sculptures are in cast bronze or aluminium and are often inspired by organic shapes such as bones, which are "complex but strangely simple". Sometimes these organic shapes transfer into his painting. For Michie painting came first. "Then, as it became more and more a tactile thing, to be touched, it occurred to me perhaps I needed to paint in the round. I started doing small sculptures and then felt more relaxed about my painting. I didn't have to worry about the tactile aspect of it any more. I mainly paint now in two dimensions."

Michie continues to sculpt. From an initial sketch he will develop an idea for a three-dimensional shape. His first aluminium sculptures were inspired by the pieces of shrapnel he found on Dorset beaches during the 1950s. The beach had been heavily mined during the war and a lot of contained explosions later took place. Aluminium is a very tough material to work and some of Michie's aluminium sculptures are quite aggressive: sculptures such as *Elegy* and *The Bed of Procrastius*. The latter is a back-to-back sculpture which resonates with the unsentimental reality of ancient Greek and Trojan Wars.

In contrast to aluminium, Michie finds bronze a more subtle sculptural material to work with. Its copper content allows him to achieve "interesting patinas, which is one of the joys of working with it". Over a number of years Michie has completed several large-scale commissions, one being for British Aerospace and another for Eagle Star. However, he prefers to work on small pieces, completing maquettes and then taking them for casting to a local industrial foundry in Bridport.

Michie has always seen metallic patina as a link between his painting and his sculpture. He sometimes uses metallic paint on canvasses to gild Roman lettering as in his *CIFG* and *GELT* paintings. Such letters are an integral part of the composition, yet they maintain an isolated identity. The letters have no meaning of themselves but are put there deliberately to achieve a harmony and balance in a composition which otherwise might become too free-floating. Often when paintings tend this way, Michie will introduce a focus element such as lettering. "I realise that when I paint a picture of that kind I work very hard to get everything correctly in balance."

Michie always takes a delight in colour: the pure invention and use of colour. Sometimes colours arise from direct observation. He recalls the time when he first came across fields of soft blue flax flowers in Dorset. "On a dull day the flowers aren't open so it's a green field, but on a good day, all these tiny flowers open out and you've got a blue field." Michie developed a whole series of paintings from these fields of flax.

For Michie all colours exist to be used. He does not limit himself to landscape colours. "The whole palette must be used, not just a corner of it. Many people are surprised by the variation." His colours range from the tonally cool and contained to the joyously warm (*Crow's Nest*). They are wide and inclusive: from the bold and flamboyant to the subtle and discreet. The result of this variation is that every painting engenders its own mood and presence. There are compositions in whites, greys and lilacs; rich reds, ochres and browns; purple, greens and blues (*Within Blue*). Some colours lie clear and close to the surface while others settle deep. Some are layered thick while others float like fine mist. Black is often there, strong and defining, as is white. Metallic paint and small touches of unexpected colour are used as accents. Brush strokes range from smooth and unbroken to fine, scratchily dry, and even hesitant.

Crow's Nest

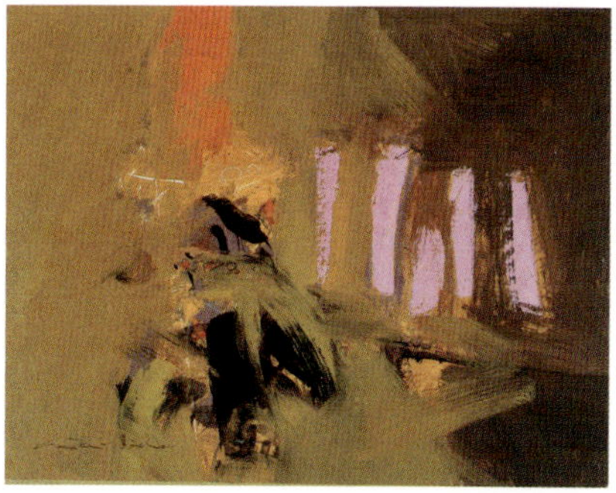

Besides a freedom in colour there is a 'particularity' in the way Michie uses paint. In his abstract work he spreads paint wide and strong. Such open areas however, are interrupted and broken-into by micro-worlds of 'scumbled' scratches and texture. Pure areas of paint are crossed by feint marks and trails. Lines are shadowed, and thin slivers cut through forms. These marks in Michie's paintings are a kind of calligraphy, his own, and he always knows where they have to go. A topographical perspective could be taken of these calligraphic marks; they could be said to relate to the visual experiences of a young war pilot, although Michie maintains that any aerial perspective is completely sub-conscious. However, what can perhaps be argued is that the precise judgement, the risk-taking and focussed energy of the young pilot continues in the painter today: "The abstract work comes from a battle, sometimes. I have terrible days when it doesn't work. I despair and decide perhaps to go back two weeks later and then it works. Some of the battles have been some of the best paintings."

In the summer, Alastair and Sally Michie open the house for a few days in the week. People come from all over the world, very often on the trail of Lawrence of Arabia or Thomas Hardy. They love the house and its interior. This is a house where on one wall a copy of an Uccello tapestry hangs, while on another are Michie's own paintings. In one room, a desk chair painted bright Chinese red sits on a turquoise rug, while in a contiguous room, a Georgian mirror hangs above dark, polished, period chairs. It is a story-book place where flagstones shine and windows are edged with shutters. Often the top halves of the shutters are closed even in daytime. This contributes to a feeling of place and people closed in on themselves. Yet, though it is a place of quietness, it is not a place of detachment.

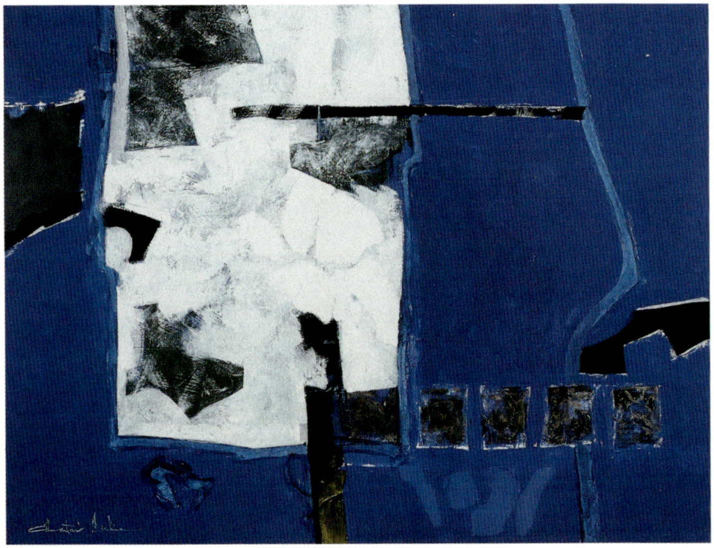

Within Blue

After so many years, Michie still feels it is a marvellous place to live and loves the house as much, or even more, than when he first came here. The Manor House, Wareham and the Purbecks are Michie's home. Here he continues to work, drawing on a fund of images from both today and yesterday. His task remains that of translating and transforming the visible world into abstract compositions which hold true to his own personal vision. He feels no need to search out new subjects. He has absorbed enough to keep him going the rest of his life. His objective remains to get everything correctly in balance, in equilibrium. That for him is the core of success in painting, and indeed in life.

Biography

1921	Born St. Omer, France
	Educated in France and Scotland
	Studied Architecture in Edinburgh
	RAF Pilot during World War II
	After the war developed a career as a graphic artist
	During the 1960s began a career in painting and sculpture
1964	Arts Council Painting Finalist
1967	Invitation to exhibit at Museum of Modern Art, Warsaw
1971	Invited by Cultural Attaché at the Brazilian Embassy, London to give a series of major exhibitions in Brazil
1970s/80s	Several major sculpture exhibitions in London, Wales and Bristol
1982	Associate of the Royal Society of British Sculptors
	Royal West of England Academician
1982	Eagle Star Properties (Winner of competition)
1984-88	Royal West of England Academy (RWA) Member of Council
1990-94	(RWA) Member of Council
1993/94	Hunting Observer Finalist
1994	Elected Fellow of the Royal Society of British Sculptors
2000	Honorary Doctor of Arts. Bournemouth University

Selected Solo Exhibitions include

1971	Richard Demarco Gallery
1990	Retrospective Exhibition, Heffers, Cambridge
1996	Mall Gallery, London
2000	Archeus Fine Art, Albermale St. London

Selected Group Exhibition include

1984-89	Royal Society of British Sculptors at Royal West of England Academy
1992-93	Alresford Gallery
1992-94	Royal Scottish Academy (three times)
1993	Members Show, Royal West of England Academy
1993	Heffers Gallery, Cambridge
1993	Beaux Arts, Bath
1993	Whiteleys - Art for Sale - London
1993	New Ashgate Gallery, Farnham
1993	R.W.A.Open Sculpture Exhibition
1993	Castle Park Project, Bristol
1993	Bruton Street Gallery, London
1993	Houldsworth Fine Art, London
1993/94	Islington Art Fair, London
1993	Scottish Contemporary Art (Phillips)

Collections

Robert Fleming Holdings, London
The Right Hon. Baroness Thatcher
British Aerospace, Filton
Oxford University
Stirling University
Watson Trust, Scotland
Scott-Hay Collection, Scotland
Museum of Modern Art, Rio de Janeiro
Museum of Modern Art, Sao Paolo
City Art Gallery, Cleveland Ohio
Royal West of England Permanent Collection, Bristol
Fife County Council
Eagle Star Insurance
United Arab Emirates
Sultanate of Oman
Art Forum Gallery, Singapore
Bp International
Mazda Motor Company
Rich and Company, London
Mitsui Bank
Art for Offices, Wapping Trust
International Contemporary Art, London
Wates Developments, London
Mecca
Sibec Developments, London
Prestige Group, London
Bournemouth University

His work is also in private collections in Europe, North and South America, Australia.

ROBIN RAE

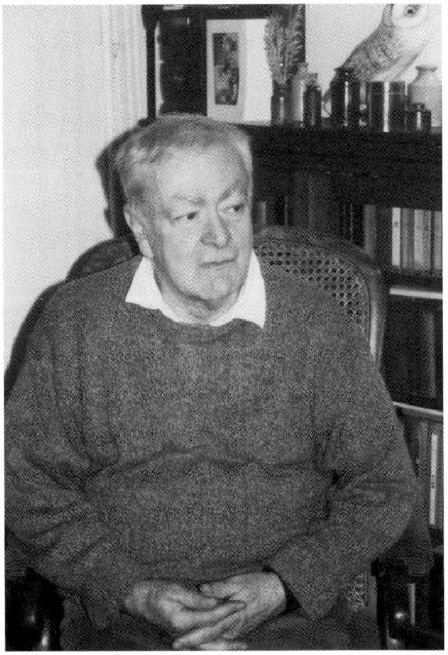

Robin Rae lives at Bradpole near Bridport. His home (and studio) is not far from the village church which stands on a knoll above the Mangerton River. Beyond Bradpole lies a part of West Dorset that is deeply rural; a landscape which consists of steep hills, hidden valleys, primrose copses, pheasant woods and single track roads.

Rae moved to Dorset in 1970, soon after which he met and married Kate. The first time he ever heard of Dorset was as a child at school. "They had a text book in Geography. It had an aerial view of Lulworth Cove and I thought I must get to see that." It turned out that his 'mind's view' of Lulworth wasn't anything like the real place. "There is the reality of the wonderful place but there's also the reality of the honey-pot tourist place as well."

For twenty years now, Rae has drawn on the Dorset landscape for his painting. When searching for a new subject it is the atmosphere of a place, rather than its physical attributes that initially attracts him. At present his paintings veer more towards the figurative than the abstract. Sometimes isolated groups of people or solitary figures inhabit his rather haunting landscapes. In a manner reminiscent of Edward Hopper, Rae's people appear to be frozen in time, self-absorbed in some event (*Beach Party* 2001). They are depicted in broad bandwidths of light which somehow transform an ordinary, everyday occurence into a dramatic affair.

Light, for Rae, also becomes the means by which landscape, objects or people (to use Paul Nash's words) 'take on a new significance', become detached, 'objectified'. Beach steps at West Bay, cast in deep shadow, become a valid subject as does *Beach Hut at Studland* (2000) or a red brick water tower (*Dorchester Old Water Tower*). The mundane can become metaphysically transformed - a painting by Rae can move beyond representation into a more visionary world.

Rae was born in London. His early school years were interrupted by the War. For safety reasons, both he and his sister were sent to the Channel Islands. However, with the German Invasion, the Islands turned out not to be a safe place after all. They escaped just in time. "Sir Hartman and Lady Lever offered to take us to Winchester, so we went to live there; they were absolutely marvellous. He'd been a Minister in one of the Lloyd George Governments. They wanted to adopt me but my mother didn't want that and neither did I. They wanted me to be an architect. Everybody seemed to think an architect was OK but not an artist."

From a young age, Rae was good at drawing. He still takes drawing seriously and appreciates fine draughtsmanship. He first decided he wanted to be an artist when, as an impressionable adolescent, he read 'Lust for Life'. "It was all about Van Gogh who grew a beard and drank beer and wine ... that was the life for me!" However, although Rae had decided on his career path he had to fight to get everyone else to agree. He remembers the 'crunch' coming with a tremendous row. However, he won, and went to Ealing Art School.

At this time in England the paintings of Neo-Romantics such as Paul Nash and Graham Sutherland were very influential. Rae liked their painting very much. He identified with the painter's search for the 'spirit of place'. In these war years the countryside not only became a home for many painters, but also their subject. In both its natural and farmed state it provided what Sutherland described as: 'an available vocabulary of forms'. For Nash, 'to contemplate the personal beauty of tree and leaf, bark and shell, and to exalt them to the principals of imaginary happenings' (Redfern Gallery Catalogue, 1937) became compelling. Such an 'engagement with possibilities', of 'incidence beyond natural appearances' strongly appealed to the young Rae. Indeed, in a review of his work at this time (1948), Helen Johnson wrote that 'with Robin Rae, one feels an awareness of the wonder and mystery of being'.

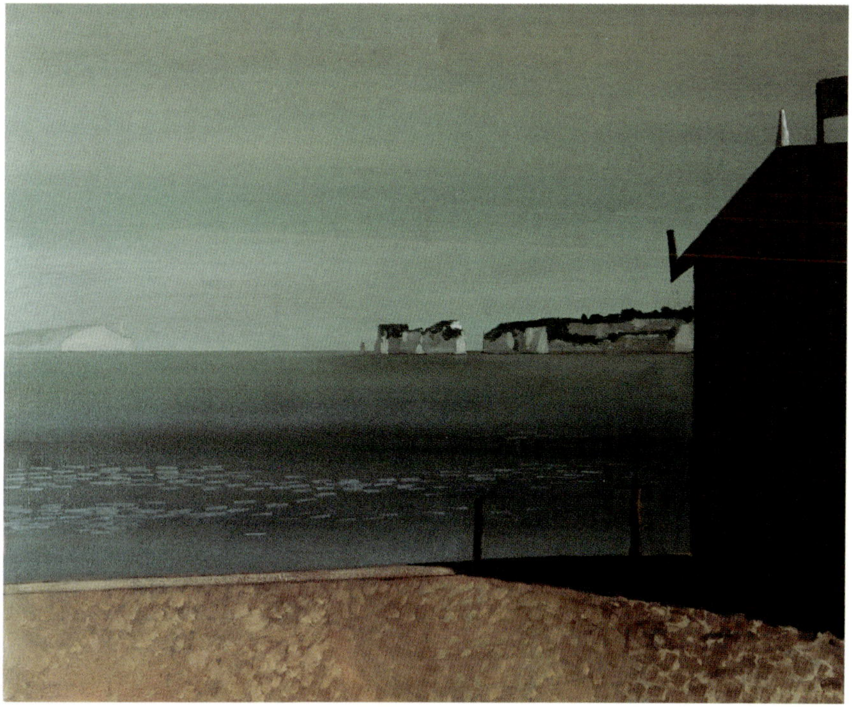

Beach Hut at Studland (2001)

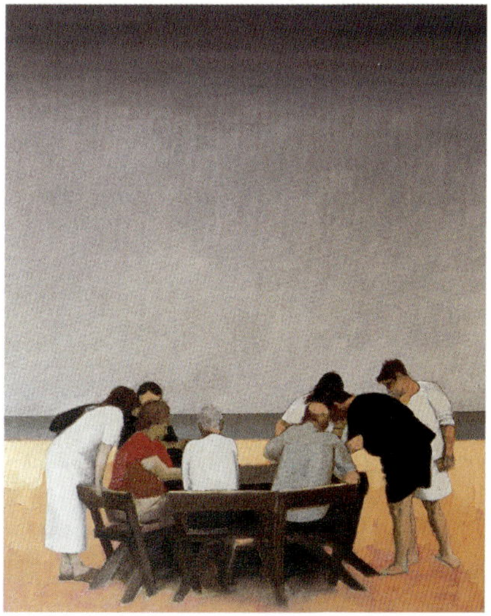

Beach Party (2001)

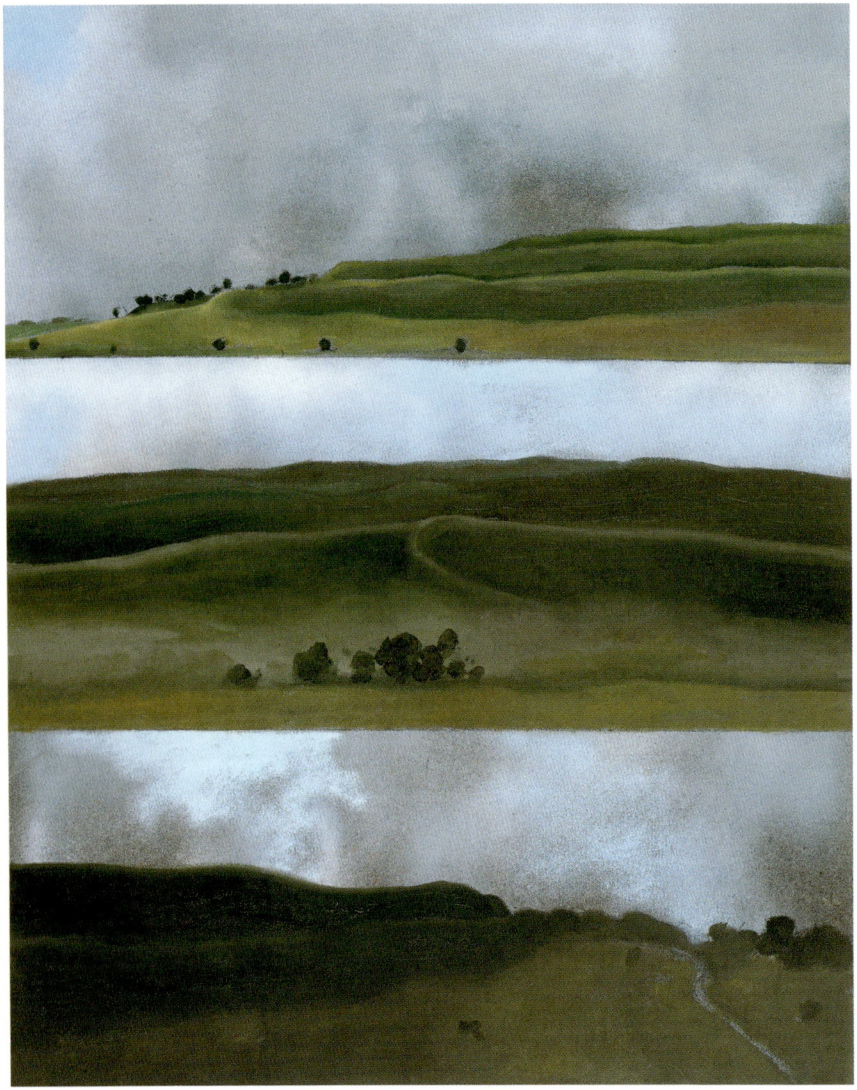

Maiden Castle (2000)

Rae was only twenty when he had his first London solo exhibition, organised by Wolf Mankowitz, the future playwright and writer. This was quickly followed by a second exhibition. Eric Newton, the then Sunday Times Art Critic, described Rae's work as being imbued with an 'uncannily vivid meaning'.

Both of Rae's exhibitions sold out, which left him feeling "rather stunned". Against much advice he decided to accept a scholarship to the Royal College of Art (1950-1953). "The staff were pretty prickly but fortunately there were some teachers whom I found most encouraging, John Nash for instance. He was just an absolutely charming man. He might see you drawing and the next day he'd bring you in a head of a pike he'd caught and thought you'd might like to draw. Then he'd show you little envelopes which he'd pull out of his pocket. He might be doing a picture with some trees here and a lake there and that sort of thing going on, and he'd say, 'I'm in the most awful trouble here' and ask what you thought about it. You couldn't really say - but that's what teaching was all about. They didn't actually teach you in the sense of techniques."

Francis Bacon, "a very charismatic person", also worked at the Royal College while Rae was there. He replaced John Minton who had been given leave of absence for a year. "Francis Bacon had his job on the proviso that he didn't do any teaching, so he was just there. You could see the door of the professor's studio open where he worked and see the

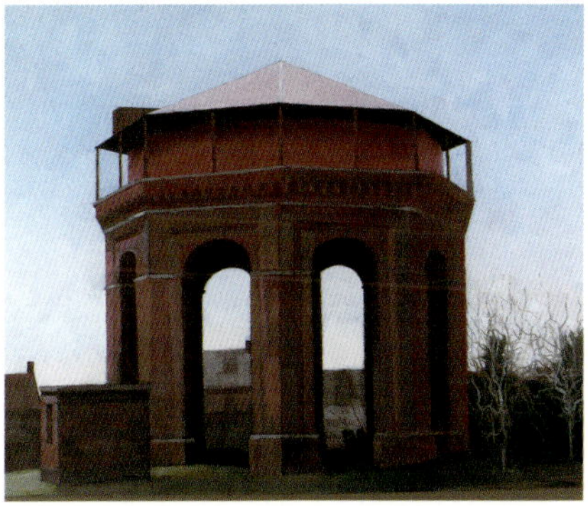

Dorchester Old Water Tower (2001)

painting of the Screaming Cardinal. Bacon worked quite furiously but he did talk to people. However, he didn't think much of any of the student's work, and was so surprised at their lack of ambition. He was electrifying. One was rather used to people saying 'you can't do that'. Picasso had done it all by now. Bacon was the first person to suggest that nothing had been done really. I remember a chap saying to him 'What about your work and the man in the street?' and he misheard him, and said, 'What about a man in the street? Nobody's painted the man in the street. Can you imagine how wonderful it would be?' Bacon was absolutely inspirational; he replaced these sorts of rural, bucolic landscapes, somewhat of Nash and Sutherland, with his own kind of painting and that of Giacometti and those sort of painters. It was rather an existentialist world which rejected all the accepted things to do with the Royal Academy and other institutions."

After leaving the Royal College of Art, Rae continued to exhibit in Young Contemporaries, Arts Council and college exhibitions while also taking various jobs to help pay the bills. In 1959, he became Head of the Etching Department at Edinburgh College of Art. In contrast to the "great intensity and searching gaze of Giacometti" he found the work of Scottish Colourists "too decorative, colourful and bonny" for him. Sickert's work was unknown there. Today his view of those working in Edinburgh is more tempered, but then he found it all a little too complacent. Anne Redpath was one of the major painters then working at the College. To a young incomer she seemed rather remote and magisterial, although others such as David Michie (Redpath's son) and Dennis Peploe were easier to talk to.

While in Edinburgh Rae painted in an Hans Hofmann, abstract way. He bought big tins of oil paint and dipped enormous brushes in. He was out on a limb but felt the need to move away from figurative work which "seemed to be running into a blank wall". Rae, like many other young painters of his generation, was deeply affected by the 1956 London review exhibition of American Expressionist painting. These artists were concerned with archetypal issues and dealt with abstraction and colour on a large scale.

In 1964, with the help of Arthur Ballard, Rae left Edinburgh for a Liverpool which he found to be both "parochial and loyal". Liverpool, in the Sixties, was a magnet for musicians, artists and poets; poets such as Alan Ginsberg, Adrian Henri and Roger McGough. Rae knew Henri very well; for Henri, Liverpool was the centre of the world. At Liverpool Rae taught Three-Dimensional Design on a Foundation course which was both "very experimental and liberating, but also, oddly enough, stultifying. We made incredible things there, including a [room size] 3D maze which Ginsberg described as state-aided lunacy."

Rae's own work at this time was abstract, intellectual and polemical. He liked the work of Thubron and Pasmore; he developed an interest in parallel perspective. He made shaped paintings, cutting out shapes from chipboard, fixing them onto plywood backing and then painting them. These abstract jigsaw works, however, retain a connection to organic forms and human figures. The backgrounds tend to be either striped or painted in a Pointilliste manner. One of these works, *Caradoc*, was bought for Liverpool's Walker Art Gallery, while another was purchased by the John Moores family. Rae frequently showed with the Liverpool Academy but increasingly found teaching too time-consuming. Also, although he was recognised as an extremely good teacher, he disliked "proselytising and persuading people to do things". It went against the grain of his character.

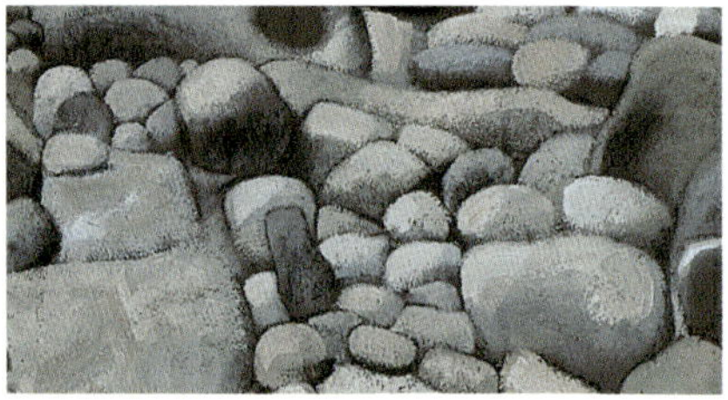

Detail *Kimmeridge* (2001)

In 1970 he decided to leave and move to Dorset. Here, he first earned a living by setting up a silk-screen printing business. At the same time, he experimented with making three dimensional objects, most of which have since been destroyed. Later, he bought a press and started etching, and then in 1987 he began painting again: "trying to forget everything I'd done before". He found he "had to go through all the sorts of period from childishness to more sophisticated painting all over again". The fact that he was now moving from abstract back to figurative was not an issue for him. Indeed, he has always maintained that as long as somebody is determined and serious in what they do one must have time for them. In 1996, Rae showed his painting at Dorset County Museum and then at Bridport Arts Centre. Since 1996 he has also shown with the Belgrave Gallery, London and The Old Warehouse Gallery, Dorchester.

Kimmeridge (2001)

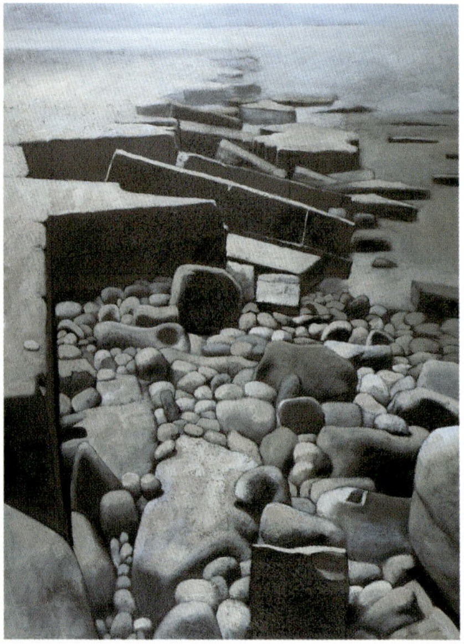

Rae paints in oil and knows how to use them, although in his self-deprecating way he says that: "What I don't know about oil paint would fill a very large library." He doesn't like acrylic as it dries too quickly for his purposes. "A lot of what I do is to put paint down and push it around using fingers; you can't do that with acrylic. Oil is like tempera, it's a special medium you either like working with or you don't." He likes the stuff of oil more than the colour of it. "I think that Bacon was rather of that kind. With Bacon the stuff is almost like ectoplasm, it emanates like a growth on the surface, although at the end he was painting flat coloured backgrounds of a totally decorative colour." Amongst other oil painters that Rae admires are Auerbach, Kossoff, Rego and Balthaus.

Today, Rae's paint is applied in thin layers. In the trackways and sky of *Maiden Castle* (2000) he has allowed small areas of the underpainting to show through. When he came to paint this hill fort he used a formula he had previously used with a cliff painting of Old Harry Rocks and Ballard Down. That is, he painted a panoramic landscape in tiered sections, rather than in the usual horizontal format. Rae prefers his work not to be framed. He likes to leave an edge of the undercoat showing on all sides: "the painting is as only a skin on the surface".

In the manner of Cozens, Rae has started to apply 'irrational' marks, with sponges and other materials, onto previously-painted surfaces. This has introduced an element of chance and exploitation and has removed any pre-conceived notions about composition. He is also searching to find an equivalent for foliage without becoming involved in natural history. "I'm not a naturalist, I'm an artist. They're different things. You have to revivify the landscape. It's what Paul Nash called the point of departure; you saw something and that was your point of departure."

The coast of West Dorset continues to be a subject much used by Rae. He has also painted on the Isle of Wight, between Yarmouth and Cowes, where "it's all marsh-land, lots of old boats, curiously Dickensian, all broken down". Like Cézanne, he argues that you can go on painting the same subject for "quite a while. You wonder whether you did it the best way so you try another. You might be very familiar with a place but having begun a painting of it, you start going through a process which is hard to explain. The painting takes over - I can remember someone saying a painting is a thing that talks to you, it starts having rights of its own and answering back to you. We all thought how funny ... but it's perfectly true. You enter into a situation where you're taking and giving, not really because you're doing it all but because the painting has necessities."

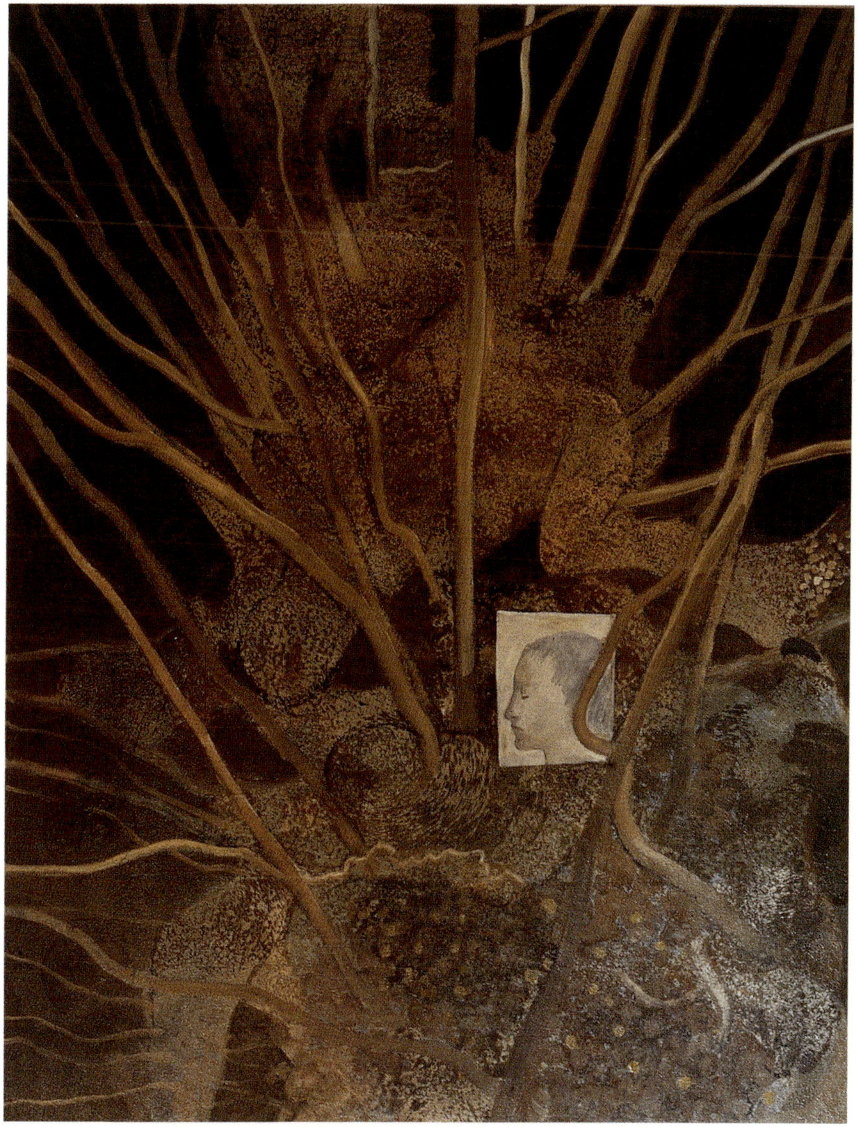

Daphne (2001)

For Rae the work of contemporary poets and playwrights is very important. He often uses quotations for painting titles. When Beckett died, Rae painted *Farewell Samuel Beckett*. He has always been touched by people leaving: "I get a lump in my throat when seeing anybody off on a train". He finds Maddox Brown's *The Last of England,* with people leaving on a boat, a heart-breaking situation. He is also very interested in Poussin's subject of *et in Arcadia ego* which he translates into many compositions. Thus he paints a car dump in a lovely romantic valley which is near by or a lady in a garden, separated and isolated from her house and home.

Rae asserts that the figure of a human being is the most difficult thing to do, yet it is a subject he never abandons. In 1948, Helen Johnson wrote that Rae's people were an integral part of the landscape and of the landscape's life; this is still true today. Rather than imposing a figure on a landscape Rae feels it should slowly form within it. Having always had a great interest in mythology Rae has recently completed some paintings based on Ovid's Metamorphoses. *Daphne* (2001), being pursued by Apollo, is metamorphosed into a tree by her father in order to escape the unwanted amorous attentions of Apollo.

Figure on Studland Beach (2001)

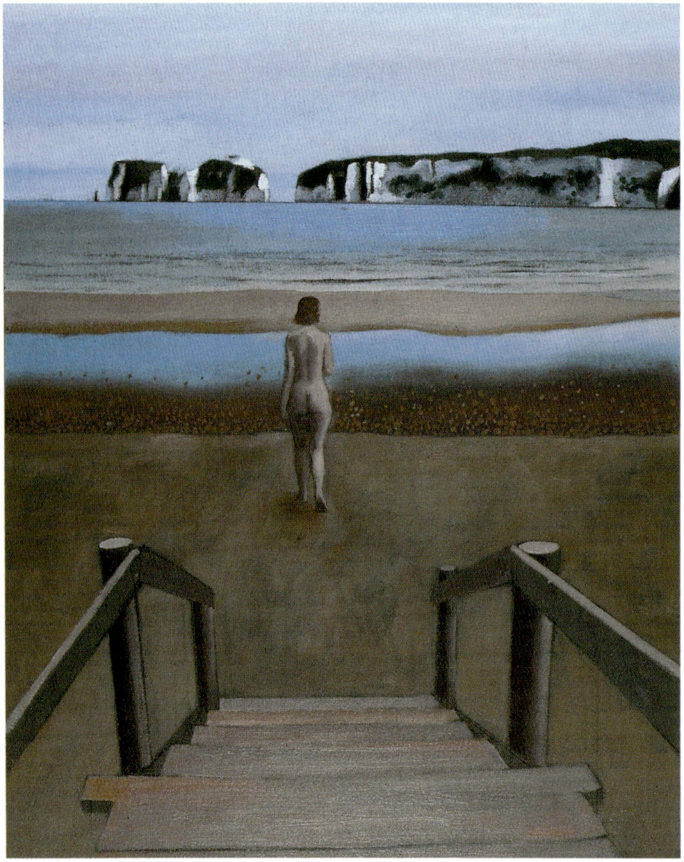

Rae intends to remain in Dorset. He still finds powerful places that pull him even if he cannot always use them. "The Chapel of Lulworth Castle is one of the most serene buildings I know. It's got a lovely, lovely feeling but I can't use that in a painting. I don't know how to. The devil has all the best tunes."

Today, Rae is no longer interested in an abstract or conceptual approach to art. Instead his concern, as stated at the beginning, is with the atmosphere of a place which he believes you cannot do "in abstract". He is a painter who, after a career of fifty years, has learned to recognise a Robin Rae painting. He quotes Gerard Manley Hopkins: 'everybody knows the taste in their own mouth'. However, for Rae, experimentation goes on. Against fashionable trends he has returned to a poetic, visionary style of painting, and in the process has made a connection to his earlier work. In the intervening years he has "tried everything, running the gamut of emotions from A to B as Dorothy Parker said". Rarely satisfied with his work, Rae is his own severest critic. However, it might do some of us well to use his criterion when judging a painting: "I've always thought that if I really like something it makes me smile, does it you?"

Biography

1928	Born London
	St. Paulís School, London (war intervened)
	Peter Symonds, Winchester
1945-49	Ealing School of Art
	Royal College of Art
	Various jobs while continuing to paint
	Head of Etching Department, Edinburgh College of Art
1963-70	Lecturer. Dept. Foundation Studies Liverpool College of Art
	Moved to Dorset, set up silk screen business
	Experimented with 3-dimensional objects
1987	Began painting again
2000	Now represented by Old Warehouse Gallery, Dorchester

Selected Solo/Two person Exhibitions

1948/49	Little Gallery, Piccadilly
1949	Hilton Gallery, Cambridge (two person)
1950	Ashmolean Museum, Oxford
1963	Scottish Gallery, Edinburgh (two person)
1968	Bluecoat Gallery, Liverpool
1996	County Museum, Dorchester
2000/01	Old Warehouse Gallery, Dorchester

* Not all Rae's exhibitions are listed

Selected Group Exhibitions

1946	Royal Academy Annual exhibition (4 times)
1947	Young Contemporaries, London (5 times)
1954	London Group Suffolk Street Galleries
	Royal College of Art (3 times)
	Little Gallery, New York (USA)
	Touring exhibition from the Royal Academy
	Arts Council touring exhibition
1962	57 Gallery, Edinburgh
1963	Royal Scottish Academy
	French Institute, Edinburgh
1964-70	Liverpool Academy Annual Members Exhibition
1993/94	Belgrave Gallery, London

Collections

Walker Art Gallery, Liverpool and many other private collections.

ROBERT WOOLNER

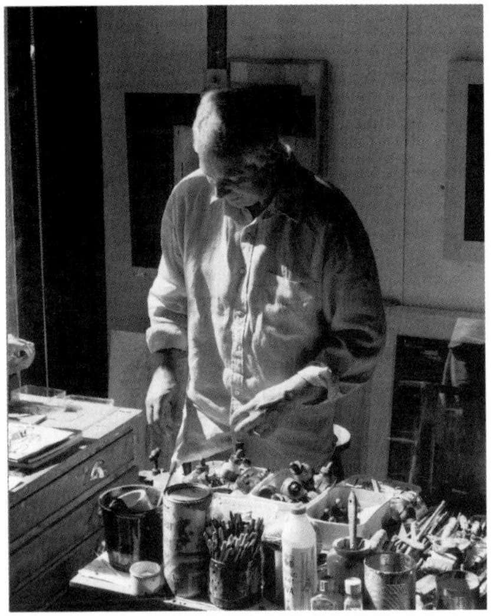

Robert Woolner was born in Jamaica. His mother was Jamaican (of Swiss and Scottish parentage), and his father Canadian. At the age of eleven he was sent to a preparatory school in England. His first memories of this country are of cold weather and fried bread, both dreadful experiences! However, he survived and stayed. Today he lives near Gillingham in one of the Blackmore Vale villages of North Dorset. The village is Stour Provost, which is situated on a low ridge of corallian limestone. Most of the older houses in this area are built of this stone, including Vanners Farm where Woolner now lives and works. The farm is no longer a working farm but many of the original buildings remain. One barn has been converted into a large studio which is lit by long vertical windows reaching from floor to eave. From the windows there are views of a rolling countryside; of neatly parcelled fields, tractor-trimmed hedges, small woods, copses, lush grass and rich brown-red soil.

Woolner's paintings over the last twenty years have shifted from an accent on realism towards abstraction. Today his work is more about incident and experience than the specific and figurative. However, he still retains strong ties to the land and is particularly affected by the strong forms found in the landscape of Dorset. Forms such as hill forts: "wonderful, powerful, moving forms in the earth which give one a very strong starting point. Such shapes are useful from a painter's perspective because you need pattern to build painting."

Within sight of Vanners Farm is the prominent hill of Duncliffe. Not much further away are two spectacular Iron Age forts: Hambledon Hill and Hod Hill. At Hambledon, the fort interior remains unploughed and the sites of ancient round huts are still visible. Hod Hill has not so successfully escaped the plough, but during the last war, ploughing did uncover two Celtic artefacts; the handle of a religious offertory bowl and the small head of a raven. Both were made of bronze and thought to have been cast on the hill itself.

Hambledon, Duncliffe and Hod Hill are for Woolner central occurrences in the landscape. He knows them well through spending time drawing there. "Up at the top there is a feeling of enclosed space. They are heavily charged environments. They've escaped ... they haven't been disturbed too much, they are condensers of history. They have a tremendous atmosphere which can vary as much as the light. You feel history, this human presence where there isn't any. It's like a horror film: the monster is more terrifying when you don't see it. In your imagination, when you're feeling it, imagining it, it's much more real".

Woolner's work is concerned not only with ancient sites in Dorset but also with the more general topography of his part of the county. Being familiar with the land in North Dorset he is attuned to small changes as well as "special times - when it snows or a storm is foisted upon you." Often when beginning a painting it is from a detail in the landscape that an idea emerges. "It might be just the way two thick trees come together in a field or the meeting point between two fields, or clouds passing behind a tree." Woolner needs very little to start with. He enjoys the challenge of "taking a small piece of information and turning it on its head". Although he draws in the landscape he would never go out and sit and paint a landscape: "the light changes the whole time. How do you paint strong light moving down through the Blackmore Vale from the top of Duncliffe Hill? It's an impossibility, although it's certainly a stunning visual sight."

Folding Light (2001)

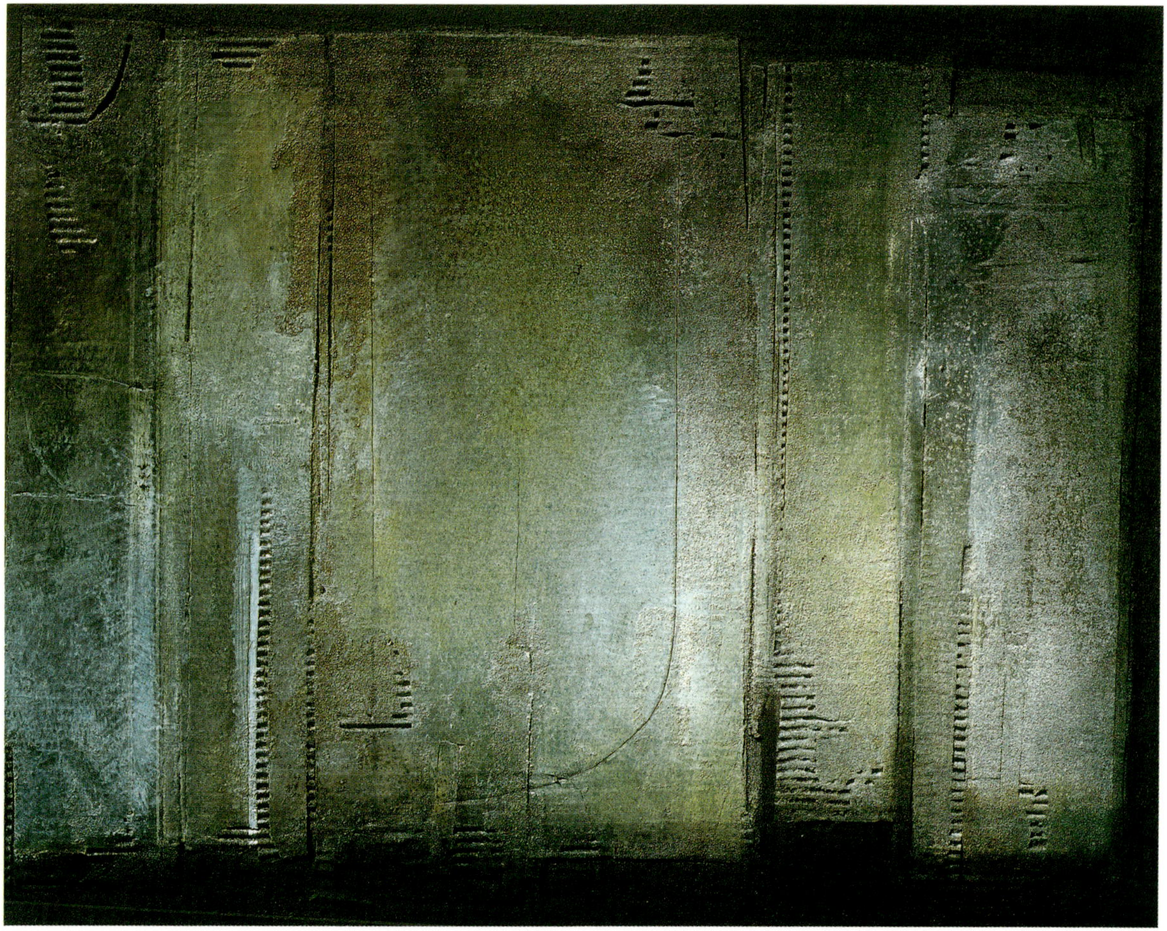

Woolner studied at Camberwell School of Art for four years. As a student of the Sixties he was excited by the avant-garde work which was coming out of America; the work of Abstract Expressionists such as Robert Motherwell, Jackson Pollock and Willem De Kooning. At that time the idea of working on a large scale was particularly exciting as "the Camberwell of the Sixties was very much Euston Road and William Coldstream". The Euston School of Painting was formal and sombre, in contrast to the colourful, gestural style of the Americans.

At Camberwell, Woolner's teachers included Frank Auerbach (b.1931) and Euan Uglow (1932-2000). Woolner remembers Auerbach working with 'tons of paint' and Uglow being 'a very, very tough draughtsman'. Both drew a great deal from direct observation and from paintings of Old Masters. Drawing was part of their core practice. For Uglow it was an indispensable discipline, while for Auerbach it offered a way to recall and capture the sense of a place. Woolner believes that "the West is not interested in mark-making to the same extent as the East. If you were trained in a different tradition, like Chinese brush painting, you'd be expected to learn so much technique."

While at Camberwell, Woolner learnt to draw from observation and today he still continues to do so. Some years ago he completed some very big, long drawings of hedges. "I took a section of hedge and drew the whole thing, in order to create an impression of an overwhelming quantity, a romantic feeling of immersion, wildness. I also took photographs as a kind of aid." Today, if Woolner uses a camera, it is for taking photographs which are interesting in themselves rather than for any relevance to painting. "If I'm up walking on Win Green, taking a photograph doesn't give me any information about the light, the space, the immensity of it all. Those things have to be confined to some kind of notation in a book as an aid to memory."

Sometimes, when drawing, Woolner will deliberately 'convert' a landscape; re-align it with an aerial perspective. "It just changes the way you see the landscape. Painting of course is a flat two dimensional process, but its flatness is its great excitement. Whatever you do, you create illusions of space. Abstract painters such as Sean Scully, Albert Irvin and Gillian Ayres work on this flat, vertical view; their work can be allied to the landscape tradition."

Light Cut (2001)

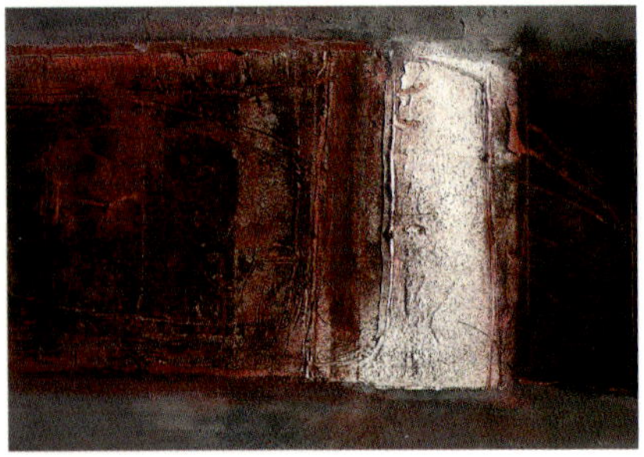

After leaving Camberwell, Woolner ran a book-selling business in the day-time and painted at night. However, as the business became more and more successful, so his wish increased to have more time to paint. Painting in France one summer he met his future wife, Mary, who also strongly encouraged him to take back the company car and to start painting - and this was what he did. "She taught, I painted, and we moved to Devon. I did a day's gardening in return for our cottage." Then Woolner was offered an Artist-in-Residence post at Canford School, Wimborne. He enjoyed both teaching and living in Dorset. Eventually, he became Director of Art at Canford and only left in 1990 to paint full-time. Today he continues to do some teaching at Vanners Studio, adjacent to his home. He likes the contact, as "painting is a very lonely occupation and teaching does focus you".

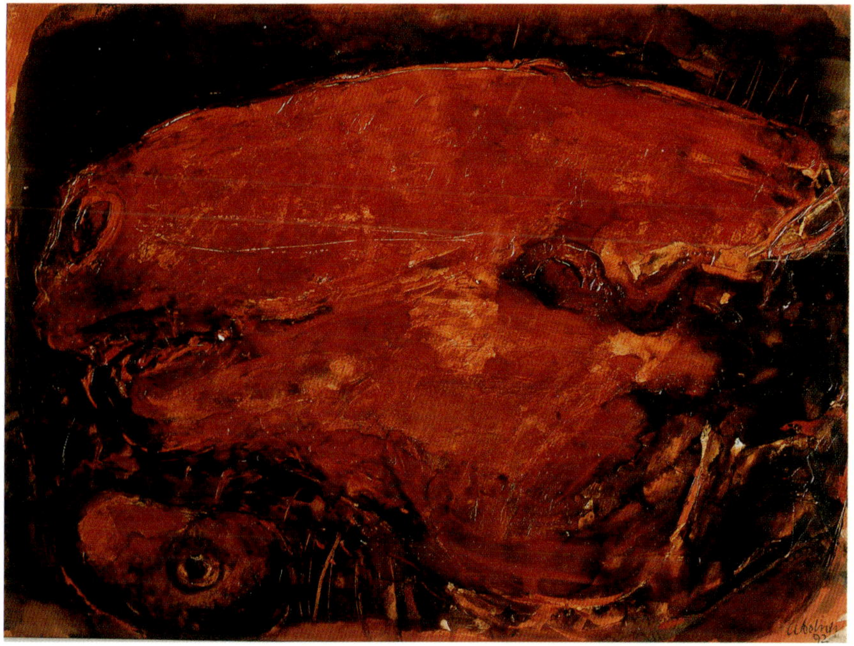

Horse Head (1993)

From his earliest days of painting Woolner has retained a strong interest in abstraction and colour. He will always be a colourist. In the early 1990s he was using very powerful primary colours; blue with orange, red with green. "In the same way that I love black and white, the idea of red and green or complementary colours has its own power. I like the idea of really using a colour and extracting everything I can from it." Such an example is *Horse Head* (1993). This was done at a time when his paintings of the Dorset landscape often contained the image of a horse in a skeletal, Sutherland way; it was 'part landscape and part horse'. The existence of a human or animal form within a landscape resonates with the work of Peter Lanyon. For example, in Lanyon's painting of *Lulworth* (1956), the white chalk is simultaneously calcified material and human figure.

For Woolner, the horse became a romantic symbol of primeval force and energy. He felt its powerful form was a good analogy for the landscape. The original horse idea stemmed from a visit to the cro-magnon caves in the Lot and Dordogne areas of South-West France: "the caves where the shape of the rock is used to help define the shape of the horse. There was a feeling of the horse and the landscape being very much part of the same thing. So, the horses grew out of the landscape and then grew back into the landscape as well. Now they've gone."

In the 1990s Woolner began to work in monochrome as an aside to his colour paintings. He has always been intrigued by black as a colour, not in the European sense of it being a colour associated with death, but in the Eastern sense. As he says: "the Japanese feel that black is the most beautiful of all colours and I tend to agree, because you immediately start to play with light when it hits black. Painting is really about contrasts: light and dark, warm and cool, hot and cold, rough and smooth, sharp and blunt. Painting as a visual language is entirely centred around contrasts. How much colour does one need in a picture?"

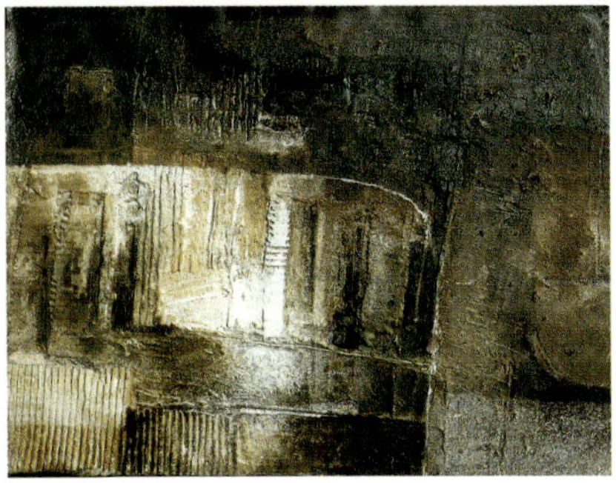

Crows's Field (1999)

Detail *Crows's Field* (1999)

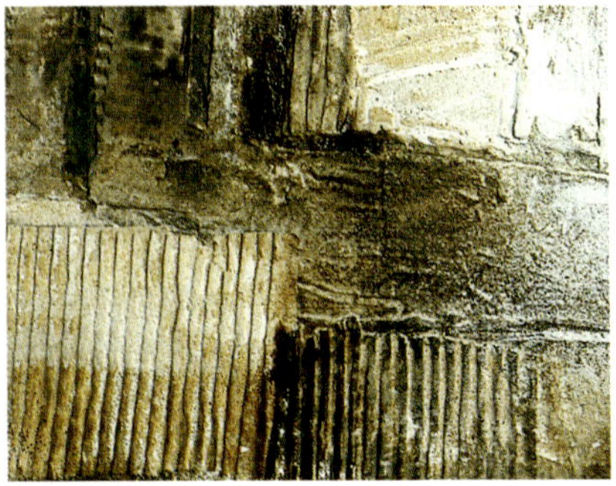

Woolner's *Crow* series of paintings, which includes *Crows's Field* (1999), are the brown, black and relief whites of earth. They take their inspiration from *The Life and Songs of the Crow* by Ted Hughes. They are perhaps Woolner's darkest and bleakest monochromatic works to date. They dismiss the image of a cosy countryside, and in alliance with Hughes speak of a place where there is destruction as well as life, cruelty as well as sanctuary, and despair as well as joy.

Today, the colours that Woolner uses are warmer and more suffuse; indeed, light itself has become the subject of his latest series of work. There is an architectural quality to many of these paintings, with their stepped corridors, planes and shadows of shifting light (*Folding Light,* 2001). In their alchemic colours they connect with the patinas of bronze artefacts and archaeological finds. Others, such as *Light Cut* (2001), and *Deep Cut* (2001) combine aerial perspective with a sliced core-view of Earth's geology.

Woolner uses both acrylic and oil, sometimes both in one painting. "Although acrylics have the advantage that they're very fast drying they don't have the richness of oil paint. There is something satisfying about the physical quality of oil when you touch it."

Since the *Crow* series, Woolner's work has become increasingly textural. Torn and cut paper, sand and other materials are embedded in emulsion and acrylic before any colour is applied. Overlapped shapes and ridges become organic forms out of which other things grow. He believes that the torn edge of a piece of paper can be as expressive as a brush mark. In his way of working with mixed media there comes a balance between control and chance, which is part of the excitement. Most of his work is on board: "I like the way that canvases have a box-like artefact character, but you can't work on them as hard as board."

Woolner tends to work in series; it helps in the exploration and development of ideas. "It's like writing one poem but producing twenty different manuscripts. It requires that you keep your energy up. It's all about ideas. Who needs drugs or whatever when you can paint?" Finally, however, "the painting has to stand on its own. It's not a word. It's nothing else. It's a complete statement of the language in its own right. It will never become the landscape. It has to fight for its own existence."

Woolner rarely throws a work away, and sometimes he will come back to a painting long set aside. Collage elements may be stripped off but any resulting distressed marks become new areas of challenge to work with. "One of the important parts of my work in landscape is the layers that happen in painting. The underlying layers can often surprise you. They give the painting a history. I think the thing about layers is that like the landscape they trap time. That's something that fascinates me. It isn't an instant process. Painting is about layers of time. A close examination of the landscape shows that it offers up its secrets, layer by layer.".

Woolner cannot see himself living much away from Vanners Farm. "Theoretically I could live anywhere. We try to travel as much as we can but it's wonderful to come back. It's where I want to be more than anywhere." Living in Dorset for him is a central part of being alive.

Recently while on a visit to his Studio, we both looked out and watched a buzzard circling high over a nearby field. After a silence Woolner said: "I think the moment you lose that sense of wonder ... you've had it really." It is this sense of wonder which leads him to work with elusive subjects such as light, but which at the same time, binds him to the ancient physical landscape within which he lives and works.

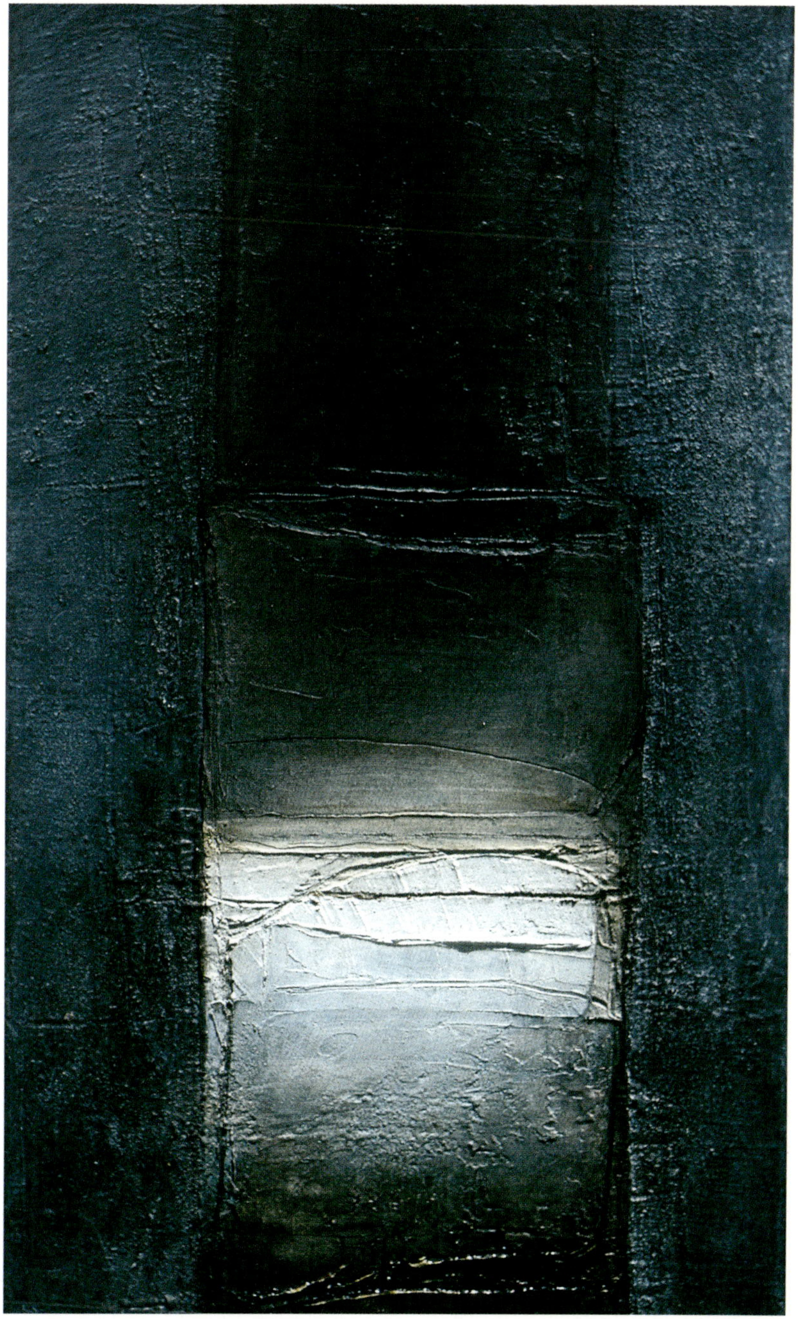

Deep Cut (2001)

Biography

1946	Born Jamaica
1964-68	Camberwell School of Art
1969	Study and travel in Italy and America
1969-72	Manager, Pulteney Books and Prints. Painted part-time. Stage designs/ constructions, Tower Theatre, Canonbury
1972-76	Painted in England and France, assisted in development of Cubertou Art Centre South West France. Worked at Islington Studio print workshop proofing and editioning, taught etching.
1976-79	Artist in residence, Canford
1978	Joined Artists from Cubertou group
1979-87	Taught at Canford, painted in Cubertou during the summer
1987-90	Director of Art, Canford
1990	Opened Vanners Studio
1990-91	Lecturer, Poole Arts Centre
1991	First Exhibition, Courses and Concerts at Vanners Studio
1991-2001	Courses in Painting, Vanners Studio

Selected Solo Exhibitions

	Butlin Gallery, Dillington House
	Anthony Brown School of Music, Canford
	Seldown Gallery, Poole Arts Centre
1991	Vanners Studio
	Dorset Art Week
	Vanners Studio
	Dorset Art Week
	British Embassy, Paris, France
	Dorset Art Week
1996	Alpha House Gallery, Sherborne
	Bettles Gallery, Ringwood
	Dorset Art Week
1998	Vanners Studio
	Alpha House Gallery, Sherbourne
	Dorset Art Week
	Vanners Studio
	Kelly College
2001	Alpha House Gallery, Sherbourne
2001	The Gallery, London (Alpha House Gallery)

Selected Group Exhibitions

1969	Northern Young Contemporaries. Whitworth Art Gallery, Manchester.
	Arts Council travelling exhibition
1976	First Artists from Cubertou Exhibition at Compton, Chichester
1979	FBA Galleries, Artists from Cubertou
	Cubertou Art Centre, France
1976-1980	Artists from Cubertou group shows in England
	RA Summer Exhibitions
	Summerleaze Gallery
	Alpha House Gallery, Sherbourne
1995,1997	Royal West of England Academy
	A Blend of North Dorset, Salisbury Library
	Seldown Gallery, Poole Arts Centre
	Quantum Fine Art, London
1999	Richmond Hill Gallery, London
1999	Bettles Gallery, Ringwood
1999	Bournemouth University Art Loan Collection, Atrium Gallery
2000	Maltby Contemporary Art, Winchester

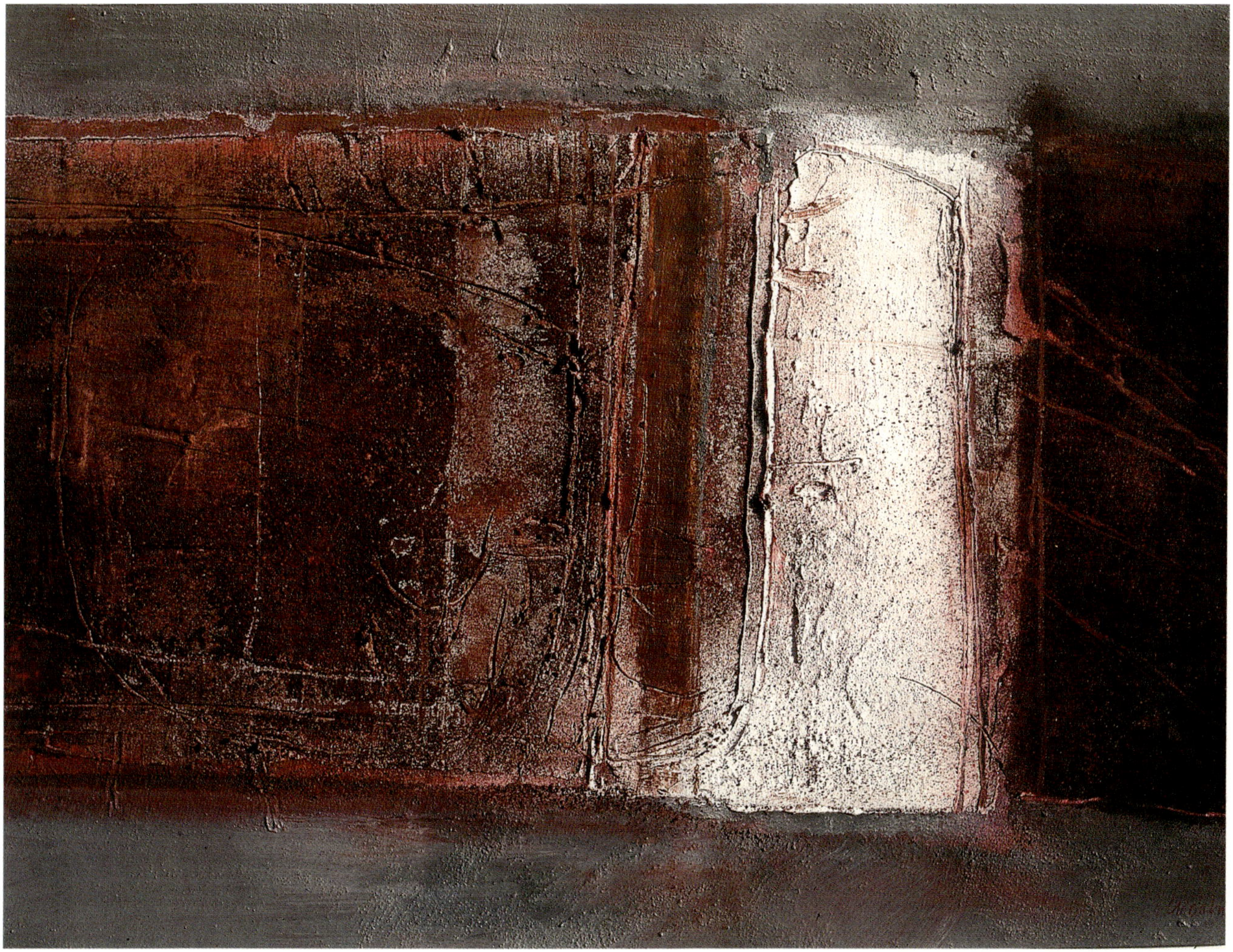

Light Cut (2000)

VIVIENNE LIGHT

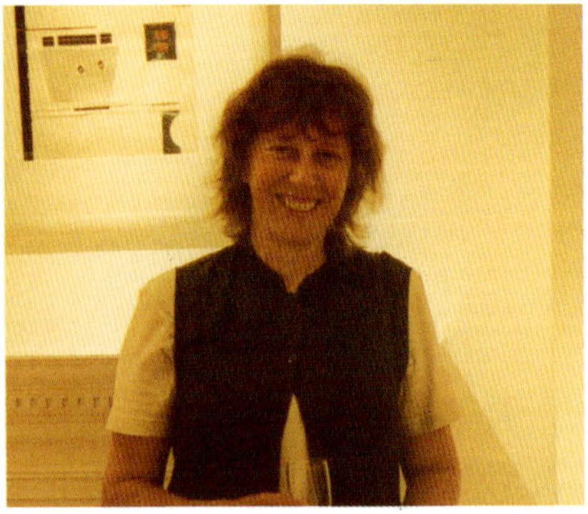

Vivienne Light was born in Dorset (1947). She is married with three children. Initially trained in music at Dartington College of Arts she taught for several years. After a Masters Degree in Education (Open University) she became involved in research. She has published several academic papers and reviewed for journals such as *Journal of Computer Assisted Learning*. In parallel with this activity she has always maintained an interest in the arts; a field in which she now solely works. She is a founder member of Paperweight (a national group of paper artists) and co-ordinated Paper Fascination (1998), an exhibition at Mino City Paper Museum, Japan. She is currently Chair of 2D3DSouth Contemporary Art. In 1995 she was elected a Fellow of the Royal Society of Arts. She continues to exhibit her work while also writing occasional magazine features and artist catalogues. At present she is working on a successor book to this volume. In her spare time she likes to walk in Dorset, play the piano and relax in Brittany with a glass of good wine!.

SARAH JANE JACKSON

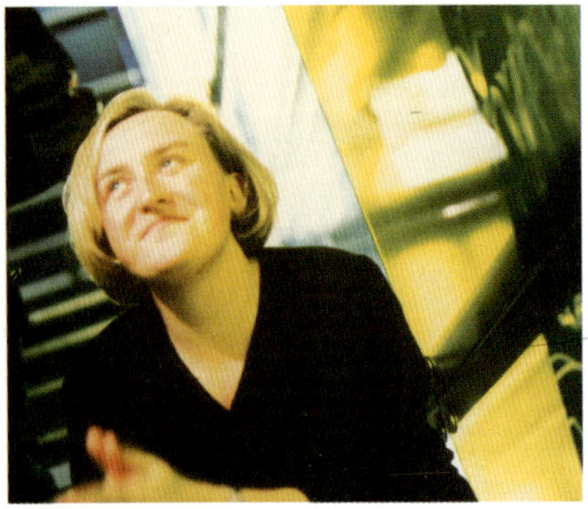

Sarah graduated in 1997 from the University of Portsmouth with a BA(Hons) in Art, Design & Media, where she specialised in typographic design. Since graduating, Sarah has worked as a designer in the field of education, firstly for the University of Portsmouth and currently as the Design Co-ordinator at King Alfred's, Winchester.

INDEX OF PAINTINGS

Martyn Brewster
Photography James Howe
Night and Day Quartet (2000) oil on canvas 51x203cm/20x80in.
Nature painting no.100, Headland series (2000) oil on canvas 122x122cm/48x48in.
Nature painting no.116, Headland series (2000) oil on canvas 50x50cm/20x20in.
Heartsong no.177 (2000) silkscreen monoprint, 2001 19x19cm/7.5x7.5in
Dorset Coast, Looking West (2001) conté/charcoal on paper 33x33cm/13x13in.

George Dannatt
Veiled Landscape - Dole's Ash (2000) oil on board 47x95.2 cm/18.5x37.5in.
Photography: George Meyrick Collection of the artist.
Poundbury Landscape (1997) oil on board 23.8x102.8cm/9.5x40.5in.
Post and Dunes (1994) oil on driftwood 29.0x37.8cm/11.5x15in.
Photography: D.Lewis. Private collection, Cambridge
Portland (1989) oil on board 69.5x59.5cm/27.5x23.5in. Private Collection
Blue Channel (1999) oil on board 14x30.5cm/5.5x12in. Private Collection

Vanessa Gardiner
November Landscape, West Dorset (1992) acrylic/collage on canvas 26x24cm/10.5x9.5in.
Eggardon Hill (1992) acrylic and collage 41x77cm/16x30in.
Harbour Coast no.7 (1997) acrylic on board 76x90cm/30x35in.
Photography: A.C.Cooper
Vertical Coast 2. (2000) acrylic on board 131x61cm/ 51.5x24in.
Photographer A.C.Cooper Private Collection
From Black Ven (1990) acrylic/collage on board 35.5cm.x53.4cm/14x21in.

Brian Graham
Photography: James Howe
Patrolled Quadrant (2001) acrylic on Fabriano paper 25.4x22.3 cm/10x8.5in.
Collection Mr. Mrs. Charles Tipper
Ambulatory (2001) acrylic on Fabriano paper 76.2x58.4cm/30x23in.
Private Collection
Landslip Hengistbury (2001) mixed media on board 20.3x22.9cm/8x9in.
Portland Inner Secrets (2001) acrylic on canvas 33x24.2cm/13x9.5in.
Collection: Mandy Bowden
Portland Revealed Floor (2001) acrylic on canvas 33x24.2cm/13x9.5in.
Private Collection

Martin Hampton - Photographer
Dancing Ledge, Purbeck
Solitary Figure - Purbeck
Eggardon Hillfort
Purbeck wall - towards Ballard Down
West Bay
Purbeck, December 2000
Kingston Russell Stone Circle
Winspit

John Hubbard
Chesil (2000) oil on canvas 147.3x127cm/58x50 in.
Cogden oil on canvas (1999) 127x152.9 cm/50x60in.
Dorset Landscape oil (1967) 165.2x203.2cm/65x80in.
Lyme Bay (1996) oil 157.5x162.6cm/62x64in.
Clouds no.2 (2000) oil on paper 69x56cm/27x22in.

Peter Joyce
Photography: James Howe
Purbeck Peninsula (2001) acrylic on canvas 127x101.7cm/50x40 in.
Windswept Walk (2000) acrylic on canvas 132.1x106.7cm/52x42in.
Winspit Gloom (2000) acrylic on canvas 30.5x25.4cm/12x10in.
West from Bodmin Point (2001) mixed media on board 17.2x15.2cm/6.5x6in.
Fishing Harbour (1998) acrylic on canvas 35.5x25.4cm/14x10in.

Alex Lowery
West Bay '148' (2001) oil on canvas 50x86cm/19.5x34in.
Photography: George Meyrick
West Bay I (1998) oil on canvas 122x264cm/48x104in.
Photography: George Meyrick
West Bay II (1998) oil on canvas 122x264cm/48x104in.
Photography: George Meyrick
West Bay '116' (2000) oil on canvas 35x91.5cm/13.5x36in.
West Bay '107' (1999) oil on canvas 46x86.4cm/16x34in

Pádraig Macmiadhacháin
Paddy's Boats (2000) oil on canvas 21.6x25.4cm/8.5x10in.
Photography: James Howe
Fishing Lines (2001) oil on linen canvas 50.6x61.2cm/20x24in.
Photographer: Andy Farrer

** all sizes are approximate*

Jack Pender's Harbour (2001) oil on linen canvas 61.2x61.2cm/24x24in.
Photographer: Andy Farrer
Pale Bay (2001) oil on linen canvas 61.2x61.2cm/24x24in.
Photographer: Andy Farrer
The Bride and Groom (2000) oil on linen canvas 81.2x81.2cm/32x32in.

Alastair Michie

Crow's Nest acrylic on paper 53.3x63.5cm/21x25in.
Margins acrylic on board 101.6x76.2cm/40x30in Collection of Susan Hudson
The Last Lily acrylic on board 81.3x88.9cm/32x35in. Collection of artist
Transformer acrylic on canvas 114.3x91.5cm/45x36in Collection of Margaret Johnson, Australia
Within Blue acrylic on board 91.4x106.8cm/ 36x46in. Collection of Bournemouth University

Robin Rae

Beach Group oil on canvas 61x51cm/24x20in.
Photography: Roger Pinn
Beach hut at Studland 61x76cm/24x30in.
Daphne oil on canvas 61x51cm/24x20in.
Dorchester Old Water Tower oil on canvas 76x61cm/30x24in.
Photography: Roger Pinn
Figure on Studland Beach oil on canvas 76x61cm./30x24in.
Photography: Roger Pinn
Kimmeridge oil on canvas 102x76cm/40x30in.
Maiden Castle (2000) oil on canvas 75x59cm/29.5x23.5in. Private Collection
Photography: James Howe

Robert Woolner

Crow's Field (1999) mixed media 56x76.2cm/22x30in. Collection of Jan Bradbury
Deep Cut (2000) mixed media 50.8x30.5cm/20x12in. Collection of artist
Folding Light (2001) mixed media 61x73.7cm/24x29in. Collection of artist
Horsehead (1993) mixed media 55x74cm/22x29in. Collection of artist
Light Cut (2001) mixed media 53.4x76.2cm/21x30in. Collection of artist

Photographic Credits

Samantha Cook: Studio Portrait *Pádraig Macmiadhacháin*
Sandra Spencer: Studio Portrait *John Hubbard*
Nicholas Hampton: Portrait *George Dannatt & Brian Graham*
James Howe: Photography for *Brewster*, *Graham* and *Joyce* paintings
(From 1983 James Howe worked at Bournemouth & Poole College of Art & Design. In 1997 he left to do free-lance work.)
George Meyrick, Roger Pinn, Andy Farrer, D. Lewis, A.C. Copper, Prudence Cumings Associates

* *all sizes are approximate*

NOTES

Brewster

1 Verlaine, P. Bournemouth, 1877 in Geoffrey Grigson *Poems and Places* Faber & Faber, 1980
2 Hardy, T. *Tess of the D'Urbervilles* 1891, quoted from Macmillan & Co., London, Reprint 1927
3 Nash, P (quotation from his autobiography) in Roger Cardinal *The Landscape Vision of Paul Nash*, Reaktion Books, London, Reprint 1994
4 Lynton, N. 'Landscape as experience and vision' in *Towards a new Landscape,* Bernard Jacobson, London 1993
5 *Night Music: Paintings and Monoprints, Martyn Brewster*. Jill George Gallery Catalogue, 1998
6 Eliot, T. S. 'Burnt Norton' *from Collected Poems 1909-1962,* Faber & Faber, London, 1963 Edition

Gardiner

7 Austen, J. *Persuasion* Quoted from Oxford University Press, 1980 edition
8 Bickley, F., 1911. 'Where Dorset Meets Devon' Constable and Co. Ltd. in *Writers on the South-West Coast,* Eric Bird and Lilian Modlock, Ex Libris Press, 1994
9 Hardy, T. 'Beeny Cliff' *in* Hardy's *Love Poems,* edited by Carl Weber, Macmillan, London, 1983 edition

Hubbard

10, 11 Munsterberg, H. *Twentieth Century Painting,* Kennikat Press, Port Washington, N.Y./London, 1951

Joyce

12 Hyland, P. *Purbeck - The Ingrained Island* Gallanoz, 1978

Lowery

13 James, M. *Alex Lowery London Magazine,* December/January 1996, pp.118-119
14 Hughes, R. *American Visions* The Harvill Press, London 1997

Macmiadhacháin

15 Macmiadhacháin, P. *The Secret Door,* 1977
16 Hyland, P. *Purbeck, The Ingrained Island* Dovecote Press, Reprint 1999
17 Bournemouth University Art Loan Collection Catalogue 2000/2001
18 Behrman, P. *The Life and loves of Pádraig Macmiadhacháin* in the Molesworth Gallery Catalogue, September, 1999.
19 Wightman, R. *Portrait of Dorset* Robert Hale, London, 1974 reprint